SCIENCE ANSWERS

Magnetism

FROM POLE TO POLE

Heinemann Library
Chicago, Illinois

Christopher Cooper

Design: Jo Hinton-Malivoire and
  Tinstar Design Ltd (www.tinstar.co.uk)
Illustrations: Jeff Edwards
Picture Research: Rosie Garai
  and Lizz Eddison
Originated by Dot Gradations Ltd.
Printed in China by Wing King Tong

08 07 06 054 04
10 9 8 7 6 5 4 3 2 1

Library of Congress Cataloging-in-Publication Data
Cooper, Christopher (Christopher Robin), 1944-
  Magnetism : from pole to pole / Christopher Cooper.
    v. cm. -- (Science answers)
Includes bibliographical references and index.
Contents: What is magnetism? -- What do magnets do? -- What kinds of things are attracted to magnets? -- What causes magnetism? -- How can you turn a magnet on and off? -- What can electromagnets do? -- Can magnetism make electricity? -- Why do compasses point north? -- Can living things sense magnetism?
  ISBN 1-4034-0954-4 (HC), 1-4034-3551-0 (pbk.)
  1. Magnetism--Juvenile literature. [1. Magnetism.] I. Title. II.
  QC753.7.C645 2003
  538--dc21
                    2003002506

Acknowledgments
The author and publishers are grateful to the following for permission to reproduce copyright material:

p.4 Tudor Photography; p.5 Jeremy Walker/Science Photo Library; pp. 6, 11, 14, 16, 24, 27 Trevor Clifford; pp. 7, 15, 18 Liz Eddison; p. 8 James Leynse/Corbis; p. 9 Martyn F. Chillmaid/Science Photo Library; p. 10 Michael S. Yamashita/Corbis; p. 20 Lester Lefkowitz/Corbis/; p. 21 Marc Romanelli/Imagebank/Getty Images; p. 22 Gareth Boden; p. 23 John Howard/Science Photo Library; p. 25 Pekka Parviainen/Science Photo Library; p. 26 Stephen Frink/Corbis; p. 28 Corbis; p. 29 Photodisc.

Cover photograph reproduced with permission of Tudor Photography.

Every effort has been made to contact copyright holders of any material reproduced in this book. Any omissions will be rectified in subsequent printings if notice is given to the publishers.

Some words are shown in bold, **like this.** You can find out what they mean by looking in the glossary

Contents

About the experiments and demonstrations

In each chapter of this book you will find a section called Science Answers. It describes an activity that you can try yourself. Here are some safety rules to follow:

- Ask an adult to help with any cutting using a sharp knife.
- **Magnets** can spoil tape recordings. Do not use magnets near videotapes or audiocassettes. Magnets can also distort the colors on a TV screen, and the distortion may not go away.
- Never connect the two terminals of a **battery** directly together. The large current could burn you.

Materials you will use

Most of these activities can be done with objects you can find in your own home. A few will need items you can buy from a hardware store. You will also need paper and a pencil to record your results.

What Is Magnetism?

A **magnet** is an object that acts in special ways. It pulls some objects toward itself and pushes some others away. These effects are called magnetism.

If you can find a magnet at home or at school, you are bound to find it fascinating. You can test what kinds of things are **attracted** to magnets. There is something eerie about the way they can push and pull each other across empty space without touching each other.

Turned-on magnet

This crane can lift metal objects using magnetism instead of a hook. The magnetism is generated by an **electromagnet,** a type of magnet that works with an **electric current.** The magnetism can be turned on and off by turning the current on and off.

Magnetism is at work all around you—in all kinds of machines and appliances. Magnetism is important to the working of **speakers,** telephones, radios, TV sets, computer disks, and **electric motors.** In factories, **motors** drive elevators and cranes. In the home they power appliances such as washing machines and vacuum cleaners. In cars they power windows and remote- control door locks. All these motors depend on magnetism.

What kind of magnet works on a refrigerator?

The kinds of magnets that you use to hold notes on the side of a refrigerator are called permanent magnets.

Inside the plastic or ceramic cover is the magnet itself. The magnet is called permanent because it keeps its magnetism, provided it does not become too hot or does not get bumped too hard. The magnet and the iron or steel of the refrigerator attract each other, so the magnet is held to the refrigerator. They can even attract each other through a few sheets of paper placed between the magnet and the refrigerator. However, the more sheets of paper you add, the weaker the attraction becomes.

What Do Magnets Do?

You can do many interesting things with one **magnet,** and even more if you have two.

Try the effect of moving a magnet next to a pile of metal paper clips. The magnet will pick up a lot of them. The paper clips are pulled toward the magnet. When this happens, the magnet is said to **attract** the paper clips. Magnets attract other magnets and some other materials. Paper clips are made of steel. Steel is attracted to magnets. It is described as **magnetic.**

The paper clips cluster around the ends of the magnet, but hardly at all around the middle. The places where the magnetic **force** seems strongest are called the poles of the magnet. The pattern of these forces in the space around the magnet is called the **magnetic field.**

Can you get one magnetic pole by itself?

Magnets are often bar-shaped. These magnets are called bar magnets. If you could cut a bar magnet in half, you would end up with two magnets, each with two poles. A new pole would appear on the newly cut face of each magnet. You could keep cutting the magnet again and again, each time producing two new poles. A single **magnetic pole** is never found on its own.

Horseshoe magnets

A horseshoe magnet is like a bar magnet that has been bent to bring the two poles close together. This shape can be helpful to attract things. It is convenient to have all the pulling power in one place. Horseshoe magnets are mostly used in school science demonstrations or in some toys.

Keeping things tidy

In homes and offices magnetism helps keep small metal objects from getting lost. A small magnet is holding these paper clips in place.

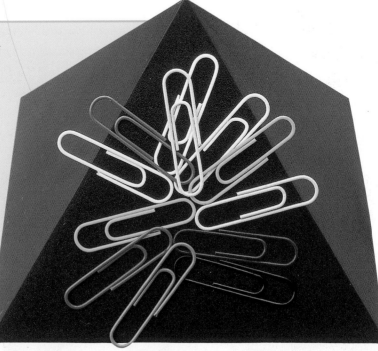

Different poles

The two poles of a **magnet** are different from each other. Hanging a magnet by its middle so that it can turn freely can easily show this. After swinging back and forth for a while, it will come to rest with one pole pointing north and the other pointing south. The same pole will always point north. The north-pointing end is called the magnet's north pole. The other end is called the south pole.

Can magnets push as well as pull?

Two magnets will behave differently depending on which poles you put close together. If you have two bar magnets, you will find that the two north poles **repel** each other. The two south poles also repel each other. The north pole of either magnet **attracts** the south pole of the other one. In other words, poles that are alike repel, unlike poles attract.

A smooth ride

Powerful magnets on this train and on the track repel each other. The train hovers above the track, giving everyone a smoother ride.
This train is called a **maglev** train, because it is *lev*itated, or raised, by *mag*nets.

EXPERIMENT: What shape is the magnetic field of a bar magnet?

HYPOTHESIS
Magnetic **forces** are strongest around the poles of the magnet.

EQUIPMENT
Plain paper, a bar magnet, some iron filings from a hardware store

EXPERIMENT STEPS
1. Place a sheet of plain paper over a bar magnet. Prop the paper up at its corners so that it lies flat.
2. Gently sprinkle some of the iron filings onto the paper.
3. What happens? Draw a picture of what you see.

CONCLUSION
The filings cluster around the poles of the magnet and form curved lines that run from one pole to the other. They show that the effects of the magnet make a pattern in the space around it.

The pattern of magnetic effects around a magnet is its **magnetic field.** The lines are called **magnetic field lines.** The iron filings make the field visible.

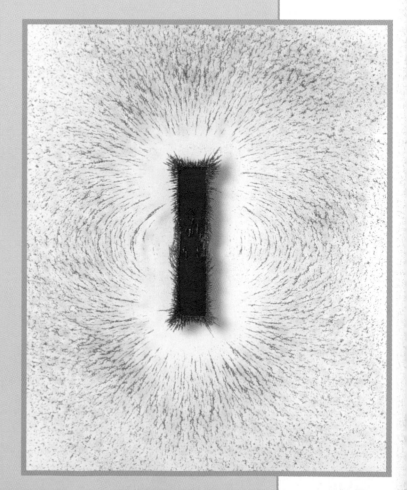

What Kinds of Things Are Attracted to Magnets?

Scientists call a material **magnetic** if it is either a **magnet** or can be **attracted** to a magnet. Iron is magnetic. Steel, which is mostly iron, is also magnetic. Most metals are magnetic.

Although a steel paper clip is magnetic, it is normally not a magnet—it will not attract another paper clip. If a magnet is held close to a paper clip, not only is the clip attracted to the magnet, the clip itself becomes a magnet. It will attract other clips. You can see this by dipping a bar magnet into a pile of paper clips. You can pull out a whole lot of clips. And the ones at the bottom will cling to the ones above them, which cling directly to the magnet. When you remove the magnet, the clips lose their magnetism and no longer cling to each other.

Recycling

Magnets can be used to separate iron and steel objects, such as pieces of scrap, from objects made of nonmagnetic materials such as **aluminum.** The iron and steel can be recycled for many different uses.

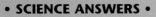
EXPERIMENT: Why are some objects magnetic?

HYPOTHESIS
Some household objects are magnetic because they contain iron or steel.

EQUIPMENT
A bar or horseshoe magnet, a variety of household objects

EXPERIMENT STEPS
1. Test household objects by seeing whether a magnet attracts them.
2. Try pins, needles, paper clips, and kitchen utensils.
3. Try similar things made of different materials—paper, wood, plastic, and other metals.
4. Try different coins.
5. Make a table of your results. Which things were magnetic?
6. Find out what materials the magnetic things were made of. Ask adults, or try to find out in books and on the Internet. Write the results in your table.

CONCLUSION
The items that were attracted to your magnet were all made of metal. Most are made of iron or steel, but some may contain other magnetic metals such as nickel.

11

What Causes Magnetism?

Magnetism exists because of the way **matter** is built. The matter in the things around you, and even in your own body, consists of tiny **particles** called **atoms.** Atoms contain several kinds of even smaller particles. Some of these particles are **electrons.**

The magnetism of a permanent **magnet** results from the combination of the magnetism of all its atoms. And the magnetism of each atom comes from the magnetism of the electrons in the atom. Each electron acts like a tiny magnet. In an atom, most of the electron magnets point in opposite directions. Their magnetism largely cancels out, but not completely.

Is everything magnetic?

Nearly every substance is weakly **magnetic.** This means that if it is placed near a **magnetic pole,** it becomes weakly **magnetized.** But it is magnetized in such a way that it is pushed away from the pole. However, this magnetism is so weak that only scientists working in a laboratory can detect it.

Iron, steel, and some other metals, including nickel and cobalt, are different. When placed near a magnetic pole they become strongly magnetized and are pulled toward the pole. When they are removed from the **magnetic field,** they may still keep some of their magnetism.

How do things lose their magnetism?

Magnetized objects can lose their magnetism. If they are heated enough or are knocked hard, their magnetism weakens. Magnets used in science and industry are made of special materials that lose very little magnetism when these things happen to them.

Why is iron different?

A piece of iron is made up of tiny areas called **domains.** All the "atomic magnets" in a domain line up pointing in one direction. The atomic magnets in the next domain point in a different direction. When the iron is placed in a magnetic field, more and more atoms swing around to line up with the field. If the atoms in a domain are already pointing the "right" way, that domain grows. Domains that have atoms pointing the "wrong" way shrink. As more and more atoms point in the right direction, the iron becomes a stronger and stronger magnet.

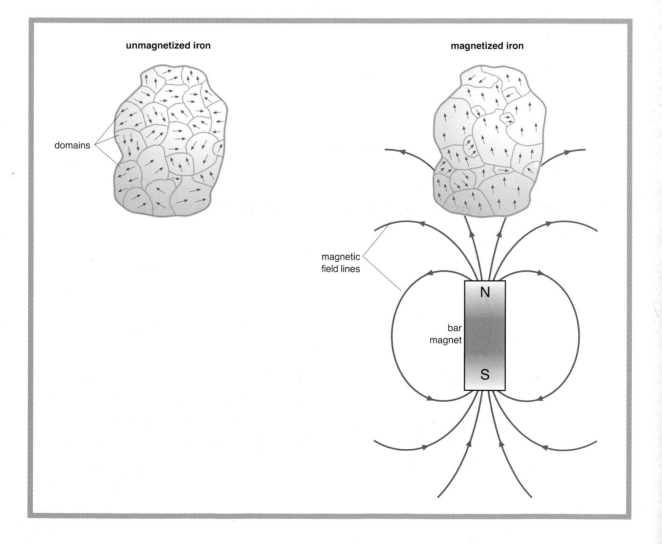

unmagnetized iron

magnetized iron

domains

magnetic field lines

N

bar magnet

S

DEMONSTRATION: Making a magnet

Magnets can be made from objects that contain iron or steel. Make your own magnet by following the steps below. You will need a long iron or steel nail or similar metal rod, a bar magnet, and some metal paper clips.

DEMONSTRATION STEPS

1. Check that the nail is not already **magnetized.** See if it will pick up the paper clips.
2. If the nail is not already magnetized, stroke one pole of the bar magnet along the nail repeatedly, always in the same direction.
3. After doing this about 20 times, see whether the nail will pick up the paper clips.
4. Write down what you saw.

EXPLANATION

The bar magnet **attracted** the "atomic magnets" in the nail and swung them around to make one strong magnet.

How Can You Turn a Magnet On and Off?

An **electromagnet** works only when an **electric current** is flowing through it. This is useful because it means that the magnet can be turned on and off by turning the electric current on and off.

How is an electromagnet made?

Every electric current creates a **magnetic field.** If you were to trace the **magnetic field lines** of a wire, you would find that they follow circles around the wire.

An electromagnet is made with coiled wires, not straight ones. The wire is coiled into a series of loops called a coil or solenoid. The field lines run along most of the inside of the coil and then come out at or near one end. They reenter the coil at the other end.

The stronger the current and the greater the number of coils, the stronger the field and the stronger the magnet.

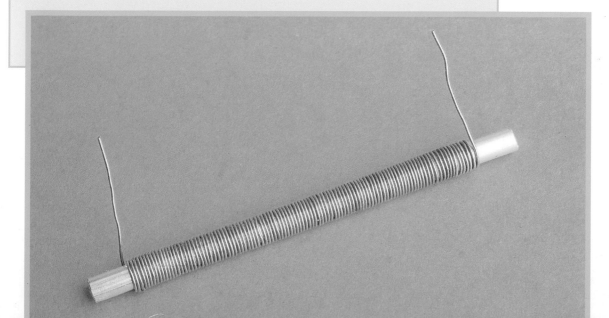

DEMONSTRATION: Making a magnetic force

An **electric current** that runs through a coil will create a magnetic **force.** To demonstrate this, you will need about 8 inches (20 centimeters) of electrical wire; a **battery** with flexible contacts; a large iron nail, 3 to 6 inches (7 to 15 centimeters) long; some pins or metal paper clips

DEMONSTRATION STEPS

1. Trim about 1 inch (2 centimeters) of plastic covering off each end of the wire. Twist one end around one contact of the battery.
2. Twist the wire around the nail, making as many coils as possible and making them as tight as possible.
3. Hold the nail over the metal objects and touch the free end of the wire to the second contact on the battery. The current will flow and the nail will become an electromagnet. It should pick up some of the metal objects.
4. Try more turns of the wire if necessary. If you feel the wire getting hot, take the end away from the battery contact for a while.
5. Write down what you saw.

EXPLANATION

The **magnetic field** of the wire coil **magnetizes** the iron nail. The field of the nail is added to the field of the coil, making the electromagnet more powerful.

What Can Electromagnets Do?

The most basic use of **electromagnets** is for pushing and pulling. Electromagnetic cranes are used in factories for lifting objects made of iron, steel, or other **magnetic** metals. They are useful in scrap yards too, where they can separate objects made of magnetic materials from those made of nonmagnetic materials.

You will find many things that use electromagnets in your home and at school. Electromagnets are useful because they can be turned on and off. They can also be much stronger than permanent **magnets** because the more coils there are in the wire, the more powerful the magnet is. Electromagnets are a vital part of the **motors** used in washing machines, vacuum cleaners, computer disk drives, and air conditioners. They are used in radios, TV sets, and telephones. Outside the home, electromagnets open and close the sliding doors of store entrances and elevators.

How can magnetism make sounds?

A **speaker** turns an electric current into sounds. The current comes from a device such as a **microphone,** CD player, or TV set. The current passes through an electromagnet inside the loudspeaker. The electromagnet shakes the loudspeaker's **diaphragm,** which is a cone-shaped piece of metal or plastic. The shaking makes sounds, because sounds consist of **vibrations,** or rapid movements, of air.

How does remote locking work?

Electromagnets operate remote-control door locks. When the driver sends a signal from the remote control, equipment in the car sends **electric currents** to electromagnets in the locks. The electromagnets move bolts inside the locks.

How do motors work?

Because an electric current has a **magnetic field**, it exerts a **force** on a nearby **magnet.** It will try to make it move. In return, the magnet exerts a force on the wire carrying the current. **Electric motors** are based on this process. In a **motor,** a magnetic field makes current-carrying wires move. The diagram here shows a simplified electric motor.

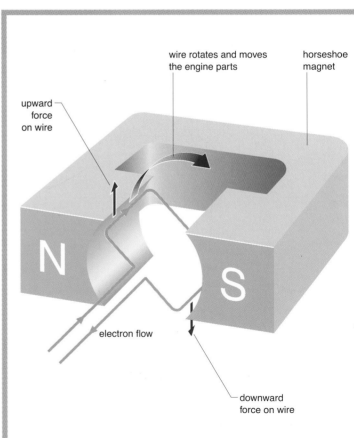

wire rotates and moves the engine parts

horseshoe magnet

upward force on wire

N

S

electron flow

downward force on wire

Magnetism in a doorbell

An electric doorbell contains an electromagnet. A visitor pressing the doorbell button pushes two metal contacts together. This allows an electric current to flow through the electromagnet. In one kind of doorbell, this pulls a metal clapper, or hammer, on a spring, hitting the bell. The movement of the clapper at the same time makes a gap in the **circuit,** switching off the current. The clapper immediately jumps back to its starting position, and the current flows again. The process repeats itself, and the clapper hits the bell again and again for as long as the visitor presses the doorbell button.

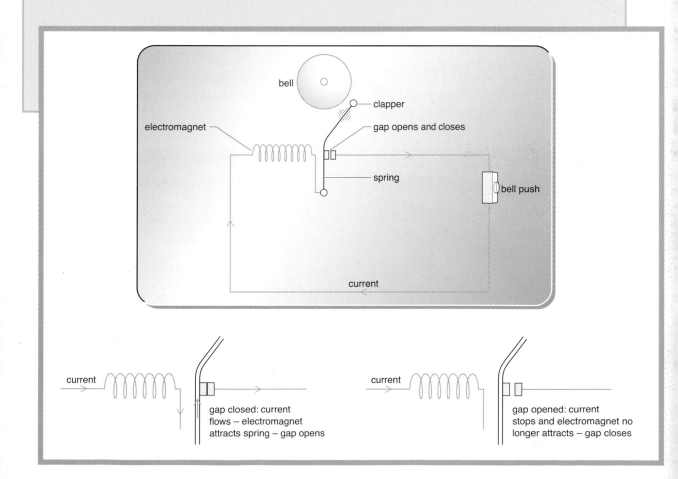

bell

clapper

gap opens and closes

electromagnet

spring

bell push

current

current

current

gap closed: current flows – electromagnet attracts spring – gap opens

gap opened: current stops and electromagnet no longer attracts – gap closes

Can Magnetism Make Electricity?

Just as an **electric current** generates a **magnetic field,** a magnetic field can generate an electric current. A magnetic field can generate a current in a wire if its strength changes—if it gets stronger or weaker. It can also generate a current if it moves or if the wire moves while the field stays the same.

How can magnetism be used to make electricity?

A **generator** is a machine that produces electricity. It contains a rotating part, or **rotor,** in which there are coils of wire. The rotor turns inside other coils of wire. In **power stations,** steam usually turns the rotor. Wind or running water can also be used to turn generators to make electricity.

Before the generator starts to work, a small electric current is sent through the nonmoving outside coils. This makes the outer coils act as an **electromagnet,** producing a magnetic field in which the rotor turns. Because the rotor turns in the field, a current flows in the rotor.

Most of the current flows through electric wires to homes, schools, and offices. But some is sent to the generator's nonmoving coils to make the magnetic field stronger, so that still more current is produced.

Changing voltage

Electromagnets are a vital part of machines called **transformers,** which make electricity safe for use in factories, offices, and homes. An electric current is carried over long distances from the power station at high **voltage.** The current flows to **substations,** where transformers change some of the current to a lower voltage for use in factories. Other parts of the current are changed to a still lower voltage for use in homes.

Playing safe

A hand-held computer game does not need very high voltage. Electromagnets built into the machine reduce the voltage of the electricity that comes from the main electrical outlet.

Why Do Compasses Point North?

If a bar **magnet** is hung from a string so it is able to swing freely, it will always turn so that one pole points north and the other points south. A **magnetic compass,** as used by hikers, has a long thin bar magnet called the **compass needle.** It is not hung on a string but turns on a vertical support.

If the bar magnet is instead mounted on a horizontal support so that it can swing up and down, it turns to point downward at an angle from the horizontal. The magnet does this because the earth acts as if there were a giant bar magnet inside it, with its poles thousands of miles below the surface. The north-seeking pole of the magnet points downward, roughly in the direction of the end of the magnet that lies far below the geographical north pole inside the earth. Wherever the magnetic compass is positioned, it follows the direction of the magnetic pull at that place.

Which way is north?

The traditional magnetic compass used on ships has a bar magnet fixed to the underside of a circular card marked with directions. The card floats on oil, with the magnet always pointing north–south. Electronic instruments have largely replaced the magnetic compass.

How accurate is a magnetic compass?

The places on the earth's surface where the **magnetic field** is strongest are called the earth's **magnetic poles.** These poles are not exactly at the true North Pole and South Pole, which are the points around which the earth rotates. Both of the earth's magnetic poles are many hundreds of miles from the true poles.

A compass needle points toward the earth's magnetic poles, not the true poles. Maps often include information about the difference between the direction of true north and the direction shown by a compass, which is called magnetic north.

What makes the earth's magnetism?

The center of the earth is called its core. It consists mostly of iron, with some nickel. The outer core is **molten,** because it is extremely hot: 8,100 to 11,000 °F (4,500 to 6,000 °C). The inner core is even hotter, but it is solid because the huge weight of the overlying rocks presses down on it.

The molten outer core acts like a giant **generator.** The rotation of the earth causes **electric currents** to flow in the molten iron. The currents generate the **magnetic field** that makes a **compass needle** point north–south.

What is the aurora?

Sometimes you can see displays of shifting, ghostly colored light in the night sky. They are often seen in the far north and south and so are called the northern or southern lights, or **aurora.** Electrical **particles** coming from the sun produce these sky displays. These particles are affected by the earth's magnetism. They travel toward the earth's magnetic poles and collide with **atoms** in the atmosphere, producing light—the aurora.

DEMONSTRATION: How to make a compass

You can make a simple compass by following the steps below. You will need a needle or long, thin nail; a permanent **magnet;** a cork or some balsa wood; and a bowl of water.

DEMONSTRATION STEPS

1. **Magnetize** the needle or nail by stroking it repeatedly with the magnet. This will be your compass needle.
2. Attach the needle to something that will float. Cut out a piece of cork or a piece of balsa wood. Tape the needle to the top of this.
3. Now float the needle in a bowl of water. It will always turn to point north–south.
4. Write down what you saw.

EXPLANATION

Your magnet acts as a compass, with one end always pointing north.

Can Living Things Sense Magnetism?

Many animals have a **magnetic** sense that tells them the direction of magnetic north or south. Their bodies have special cells that contain **crystals** of the iron mineral magnetite. The crystals act as compasses, turning to line up with the earth's **magnetic field.** Nerve signals from the cells carry this information to the animals' brains.

What is the range of the magnetic sense?

Mole rats dig tunnels up to 656 feet (200 meters) long, aided by their magnetic sense. Young newts use their magnetic sense to find their way to their home pond from distances of as much as 9 miles (15 kilometers). Birds and many ocean-dwelling species **migrate** distances of thousands of miles, using the earth's magnetism and other clues to guide them.

Guided by magnetism

Loggerhead turtles nest on the coast of Florida. When young ones hatch, they swim out to sea and begin a five- to ten-year journey 8,080 miles (13,000 kilometers) clockwise around the Atlantic Ocean. Laboratory experiments have shown that the earth's magnetic field guides them.

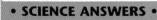
EXPERIMENT: How can you show the effects of the earth's magnetism?

HYPOTHESIS

You can imitate the earth's magnetism by making a model. (NOTE: a compass needle will be horizontal at the magnetic equator; angle of dip is the angle, or space, between the horizontal and the direction of Earth's magnetic field)

EQUIPMENT

small bar **magnet,** modeling clay, small compass

EXPERIMENT STEPS

1. Use a bar magnet, or **magnetize** a short nail or other metal rod as described on page 14. Press it into the center of a ball of clay.
2. Move the compass around near the ball of clay to see the direction of the magnetic field.
3. Notice the following:
   a. how the angle of dip varies over the surface
   b. where the **magnetic poles** are
   c. magnetic equator
4. Write down what you saw.

CONCLUSION

The angle of dip is different on different parts of Earth's surface.

People Who Found the Answers

William Gilbert (1544–1603)

William Gilbert was the personal doctor to Queen Elizabeth I and King James I. He was the first person to realize that the earth is a giant **magnet.** He performed many experiments with **lodestones.** Studying how a compass needle behaved near a lodestone convinced him that the earth is a giant magnet. He wrote the first great English scientific book, *The Magnet.* Gilbert invented the term ***magnetic pole.*** He was one of the earliest English scientists to believe that the earth and planets travel around the sun. He believed, wrongly, that magnetism holds the planets in their paths around the sun. He also studied electricity and clearly realized its differences from magnetism.

Hans Christian Oersted (1777–1851)

Danish scientist Hans Christian Oersted was the first to find the long-suspected connection between magnetism and electricity. Oersted made his great discovery during a lecture to students in 1819. He was moving a **magnetic compass** near a wire carrying an **electric current** when he noticed a slight turning of the **compass needle.** He went on to study the **magnetic** effects of the current on all kinds of materials and showed that the current was truly producing magnetism. His discovery created a sensation among scientists. As a result, within a few years others had discovered how to make the first **electromagnets** and **electric motors.**

Amazing Facts

- The earth's **magnetic field** has flipped direction many times in the past. In just a thousand years or so, the strength of the field falls to zero and then builds up again in the opposite direction. The last time the earth's north and south magnetic poles swapped places was about 700,000 years ago.

- Everything has some magnetism, but in the case of most objects it is millions of times weaker than the magnetism of compass needles and similar objects. This means that most things are affected by magnetic fields by a very small amount. Dutch scientists have been able to make objects levitate, or float in the air, using very strong magnetic fields. They have done this with drops of water, vegetables, and even a living frog—which was unharmed.

- A magnet falls more slowly through a metal tube than a nonmagnetic object does. As the magnet falls, each part of the metal tube feels the strength of its magnetic field changing. This changing field disturbs the **electrons** in the **atoms** of the metal and sets up electric currents in the metal. These currents have magnetism that acts on the magnet, slowing it down.

Glossary

aluminum light silvery metal that is not magnetic

atom one of the small particles that matter is made of. An atom is made of smaller particles, including electrons.

attract/attraction pull without touching, as a magnet pulls metal objects and the earth pulls objects down toward itself

aurora area of glowing colored light in the sky, most often seen in the far north and south

battery device that generates electric current by a chemical reaction

circuit arrangement of electrical components through which a current can flow to do some job

compass needle light thin bar magnet used in a magnetic compass

crystal type of material in which the atoms are arranged in an orderly pattern

diaphragm thin plate of material, such as metal or plastic. A vibrating diaphragm is important in a speaker.

domain tiny region of a material in which all the atoms are pointing the same way so that their magnetic fields add together

electric current stream of electrons or other particles. The current has a magnetic field and can produce heat or light.

electric motor machine that uses an electric current to produce motion

electromagnet device that develops a magnetic field when an electric current is passed through it

electron particle found in every atom. Most electric currents are a flow of electrons.

force influence that pushes or pulls an object

generator machine for producing an electric current. It is usually driven by steam.

lodestone natural magnet

maglev abbreviation for *magnetic levitation. Levitation* means "lifting." Maglev vehicles are lifted above a track by the force between electromagnets in the vehicle and in the track.

magnet object that can attract certain metals, such as iron

magnetic describes a material that either is, or can be made into, a magnet

magnetic compass device containing a light magnetized rod, or needle, that is free to turn to point toward the earth's magnetic poles

magnetic field pattern of magnetic influence around a magnet

magnetic field lines imaginary lines that show the direction of a magnetic field at each point in space

magnetic pole part of a magnet where the magnetic field is strongest

magnetize to turn an object made of magnetic material into a magnet

matter anything that has mass and occupies space

microphone device that detects sounds and produces an electric current, which can be used to produce copies of the original sounds at another time or place

migrate/migration regular movement of animals in search of food or breeding places

molten melted and at high temperature

motor machine that produces motion, either from electricity or by burning a fuel such as gasoline

particle very small piece of matter

power station plant where electrical power is produced

repel to push away, often without touching. Similar poles of different magnets repel each other.

rotor rotating coil in an electric motor or generator

speaker device that produces sound using the electric current from a radio, TV, telephone, or other such device

substation place where transformers change the voltage of electricity—for example, reducing it to make it safer to use in the home

transformer device for changing electrical voltage

vibration rapid backward-and-forward motion

voltage push that makes an electric current flow

Index

More Books to Read

Fullick, Anne and Chris Oxlade. *Science Topics: Electricity and
    Magnetism*. Chicago: Heinemann Library, 2000.

Tiner, John Hudson. *Magnetism*. Mankato, Minn.: Smart Apple
    Media, 2002.

Tocci, Salvatore. *Experiments With Magnets*. Danbury, Conn.:
    Children's Press, 2001.

SALT BLOCK COOKING

SALT BLOCK COOKING

70 Recipes for Grilling, Chilling, Searing, and Serving on Himalayan Salt Blocks

MARK BITTERMAN

Recipes by Andrew Schloss and Mark Bitterman
Photography by Mark Bitterman

Andrews McMeel
Publishing®

Kansas City · Sydney · London

Andrews McMeel Publishing, LLC
an Andrews McMeel Universal company
1130 Walnut Street, Kansas City, Missouri 64106

www.andrewsmcmeel.com

14 15 16 17 SHO 10 9 8 7 6 5

ISBN: 978-1-4494-3055-9

Library of Congress Control Number: 2012955065

Design: Holly Ogden
Photography: Mark Bitterman
Photo Credits: Ejaz Ahmad, pages vii, 6 (both), 7 (top),
8 (top); Zohaib Akhtar, page 7 (bottom); Maqbool Bhatti,
pages 8 (bottom), 9, 11; Andrew Schloss, page 67
Food Stylist: Adrian Hale
Prop Stylist: Pamela Fabrega

ATTENTION: SCHOOLS AND BUSINESSES

Andrews McMeel books are available at quantity
discounts with bulk purchase for educational, business, or
sales promotional use. For information, please e-mail the
Andrews McMeel Special Sales Department:
specialsales@amuniversal.com

CONTENTS

ACKNOWLEDGMENTS

My laptop doesn't contain enough ink to thank my dear friend Andy Schloss for his culinary prowess and writerly professionalism in crafting the recipes for this book. Profound thanks to my editor, Jean Lucas, who has shown inordinate grace and wisdom in dealing with me. Thanks also to the rest of the crew at Andrews McMeel, most especially to Holly Ogden for her beautiful book design work, and to Kirsty Melville for believing in this book and publishing it. Thanks also to my excellent agent, Lisa Ekus, for her faith and friendship.

Thank you, Adrian Hale, for your calm acumen and beautiful hands (literally and figuratively) in food styling. My gratitude to Pamela Fabrega for all the hustle and creativity: I still owe you a tank of gas. Additional styling thanks to Kierstin Buchner, Ellen Jackson, and Delores Custer for your hard work and good counsel. Thank you, Leela Cyd, for contributing your excellent graphical eye. My thanks to Mark Fitzgerald for photo-editing help. Thank you, Pete Perry, for your generosity on all fronts photographic.

Deep thanks to the indomitable Melissa Smith at The Meadow for holding down the fort during my absences while writing. I am ever grateful to Mark Chapman, Violet Tchalakov, Kristen Cooper, Kayla Carlson, Linda Le, Nicole Alden, Kimberly Silman, Jordan Frand, Jamie Swick, Nick Raz, Jaime Newman, Annette Strean-Cornelius, Arturo Martinini, and the rest of the brilliant staff at The Meadow for their passion and hard work spreading the good word of salt.

Thank you to my friends in Pakistan: Maqbool, Ejaz, Mian, Zohaib, Akhtar, and others. Thanks to Matt, Caitie, Poppy, Fiona, and Cecilia Coleman for lending me your home (and yourselves!), and also to Miriana, Matt, and Mike Clark for the stepladders and dinners along the way. Thanks to the many bighearted people who sent me pictures and ideas for cooking over the years.

Most of all, I thank my two beautiful and brilliant boys. Austin, your quick humor and wily playfulness help me to see the truth in myself; and Hugo, your high-octane curiosity and boisterous affection are my keenest reminders of the awesome vitality of the human spirit.

INTRODUCTION

"Here in this wholly mineral
landscape lighted by stars like
flares, even memory disappears."
—Paul Bowles, *Their Heads Are Green and Their Hands Are Blue*

A boulder of rock salt emerges from darkness of a sixteenth-century mine-shaft in Pakistan and explodes into light, catching and refracting the sun. Gaze into the deep ferrite glow of a massive block of Himalayan salt, and glimpse the unfathomed history of our planet. This salt was formed in the Precambrian era, about 600 million years ago, as a great inland sea evaporated, leaving behind a massive salt deposit. Sedimentary and tectonic activity sealed the salt in a hermetic vault, and buried it deep. As stars died and formed in the celestial sphere above, and the continents scattered, collected, and scattered again, the ancient salt bed abided under the intense pressure and heat of the earth.

Meanwhile, the percolating eukaryotic cells that composed all life on earth evolved into shellfish and trilobites. Fish found flippers and began swimming through the sea, great fern forests emerged on land, and then came the reptiles. Still the salt glowed darkly in the depths of the earth. Dinosaurs grew to towering heights, mammals peeked from beneath the leaves, and birds took flight. Grazing and carnivorous mammals, and then primates, took hold, and still the salt remained in darkness. And all the while, slowly at first, then more rapidly, over countless lost ages, the rock encasing the ancient seabed rose up and up.

Marl, dolomite, gypsum, and shattered igneous formations broke and churned as they rose, until at last the long-lost crystallized sea broke free, surrounded by peaks that licked the rarified air at the rim of the sky and cast shadows over valleys below.

Half a billion years after the internment of the salt deposit, man appeared, gawking at the heavens and whittling spears, then scattering across Asia and beyond. One lovely evening 1.8 million years later, in 326 BC, Alexander the Great gave his troops a rest in the Khewra area of what is now Pakistan. An observant fellow noted in his diary that the horses were taken with licking the rocks—and thus salt was discovered. Some eighteen centuries later, Jalaluddin Muhammad Akbar was born. At the happy age of thirteen, the boy lost his father, who fell to his death from the library stairs, and Akbar ascended to become the greatest Mughal emperor. Akbar's two lasting contributions to posterity were the vast accessioning of art from around the world into the Mughal collections and the introduction of standardized salt mining at Khewra, the present-day site of Alexander's discovery.

Tracing the history of our own biological development, this salt is rich in iron, calcium, and 80 other trace minerals—all the trace minerals present in your body, and in remarkably similar proportion. The best grades of Himalayan salt are mined by hand in the same way they were under Akbar. Choice boulders, sometimes weighing in excess of 500 pounds, are sliced into cubes, platters, planks, and chunks for use at your table.

I first heard about salt blocks from a lovely and irrepressibly energetic couple, Laura Castelli and Jerry Petrozelli, who had recently started selling them to chefs. They gave me a tour of their warehouse, and I found myself licking salt dust off the stone saw that they used to cut blocks into specified dimensions.

As I started using salt blocks at home, it quickly became apparent that the few forward-thinking chefs using salt blocks to sear Wagyu steak or season ahi tuna were only scratching the surface. By the time I began importing them for my business and selling them, I was preparing aioli, salads, steak tartare, and ceviche on salt plates and in salt bowls. My frying pans gathered dust as I cooked fajitas, johnnycakes, duck breasts, and whole fish on salt blocks. The more I shared ideas with others, the more I learned. Curing fiends came to me with preserved lemons, watermelon prosciutto, beef leather, and mushroom pickles! I found myself warming salt blocks and bowls for dishes like chocolate fondue, bagna cauda, and raclette. In the winter, I'd chill a block to make peanut brittle and salted caramels, or sip warm sake from cups lathed out of salt. Come summer I'd freeze blocks to make ice cream and gremolata, and treat friends to chilled salt cups filled with frozen mint juleps. The more I cooked with them and ate from them, the more amazed I became.

And I am still amazed. Salt block cooking shines like a new star in the sky, a beacon for anyone who enjoys fun, flavor, and discovery in cooking.

The New Kitchen Essential

Salt blocks are the boldest new idea in cooking since the matchstick. The non-stick pan, the induction range, and sous-vide immersion circulators are certainly amazing examples of modern cooking technology, but in the grand scheme of things they are merely improvements in convenience, efficiency, and technique. From the first stone griddle to pans sculpted from clay to skillets hammered from copper, virtually every technology for cooking ever invented is predicated on the belief that food is separate from the vessel that cooks it. Salt blocks are an imaginative leap into a bold, bright, Disney-esque world where the things we cook and the things we cook them on dance gracefully together.

Salt blocks can cook, cure, cool, freeze, caramelize, brown, soften, firm, crisp, and show off food while making it more digestible and flavorful. The salts in a salt block react differently with food depending on the moisture, fat, sugar, starch, and protein content of the food, the temperature of the salt, and the length of time the food is in contact with the salt. Fortunately you don't need to think about all of this every time you unpack your salt blocks. With a few basic, easy-to-remember principles in hand, you can bend all the mind-blowing power of salt blocks to your every whim. Salt blocks may not be the most high-tech piece of cooking equipment in your kitchen, but they can transform food unlike anything else.

Properties

Himalayan salt can range in color from perfectly clear to mellow amber-yellow to feisty meaty red to silver-blue Waterford crystal. The colors are allopathic, meaning they come from various trace minerals trapped in the salt crystal matrix: iron, magnesium, copper, potassium, and dozens of others. Every mineral in the earth's crust plays a role in the cast of characters.

Himalayan salt blocks have very little porosity, and because they have virtually no residual moisture (.026 percent), they can be safely heated or chilled to great extremes. I've tested them up to 700°F (370°C), which is hotter than most pizza ovens. Salt doesn't melt until 1473.4°F (800.8°C), so there is still plenty of opportunity to increase the temperature more, though I'm at a loss as to what culinary benefit that might offer.

You can also cool salt blocks. You can put them in the freezer and take them down to 0°F. If that doesn't do the job to your satisfaction, you can immerse them in liquid nitrogen, and cool them down to −321°F (−196°C). At that temperature some rare classes of materials become superconductive, transmitting and storing electricity with no resistance and exhibiting weird magnetic properties that allow them to levitate. Lack of evidence has led me to realize that I will probably never discover some exotic new law of physics with my subzero salt

block (physicists have already probed those options better than I could), and so I have settled for just making flash-frozen salted meringue.

Salt's specific heat capacity (the amount of heat required to change the temperature of 1 kilogram of a substance by 1 degree) is 3.31 kJ/kg K (0.79 Btu/lb °F). Copper, by comparison, is just 0.385 kJ/kg. In other words, when it comes to heat retention, salt blocks make your momma's heavy old cast-iron skillet—or any other skillet you have in your kitchen—seem like aluminum foil by comparison. No disrespect, Momma.

Two other considerations come into play when working with Himalayan salt plates. It's counterintuitive, but a huge flat block of salt actually delivers salt to food in a very modest, deliberate, and measured fashion. A salt block's lack of porosity means that it has only one surface to offer food, compared to the multitudes of facets in a crystal of granular salt. Because a salt block has only one solid surface that's in contact with your food, it dissolves slowly and imparts its seasoning in a moderate way. Second, the high quantity of trace minerals in salt blocks (1.2 percent sulfur, 0.4 percent calcium, 0.35 percent potassium, 0.16 percent magnesium, and 80 other trace minerals) mitigates the full-frontal saltiness of pure sodium chloride, so the actual salt flavor that salt blocks impart is milder and more balanced than that of granular salt—and by extension it elicits more complex flavors from your food.

Provenance

There are a number of mines producing Himalayan salt blocks, but none of them are in the Himalayas. For this bit of confusion (yes, it is sort of an anticlimax), we thank the early promoters of the beautiful pink rock salt from Pakistan, who seemed to have felt that the word *Himalayan* had more curb appeal than *Punjabi* or *Pakistani*. There are indeed salts produced in the Himalayas, but none of them are commercialized outside the region—after all, why would you pay to transport the heaviest food we eat from the world's tallest and most inaccessible lands when you can just make it at sea level?

No, Himalayan salt as we know it harkens from the less glorious-sounding but very aptly named mountains called the Salt Range, almost 200 miles from the southernmost scarp of the Himalayas, in Pakistan. But once a term enters our lexicon it's hard to dislodge it, so rather than calling it Salt Range salt or even Pakistani pink salt (which I tried to popularize with little success), we'll stick with the popular term.

Pakistan is home to more than 170 million people, who speak more than sixty languages. The north of the country boasts incredibly beautiful mountains that dwarf those of Switzerland or Colorado. It is home to five of the world's majestic 8,000-meter peaks and to more than fifty that are above 7,000 meters. The Himalayas they are not, but the Salt Range is nonetheless ruggedly beautiful. The tallest mountain here is Sakaser, standing 4,993 feet (1,522 meters). The word *Sakaser* suggests a meaning along the lines of "Buddha pond," so named because it presides over a 2½-mile-long salt lake at its base. Sakaser stands at the head of the Soan Sakaser Valley, where a number of salt lakes nourish salt-resistant shrubs that serve as a delicacy for passing camels.

There are six principal salt mines in the Salt Range. The largest and most famous is the legendary Khewra Salt Mine (occasionally referred to as the Mayo Salt Mine), which extends along twenty-five miles of tunnels in eighteen working levels. The government estimates the mine holds about 6.7 billion tons of salt, though this number is debated. The mining process follows a model established in 1827 by a British engineer who proposed excavating rooms out of not more than 50 percent of the salt in the seam and leaving the other 50 percent behind to serve as pillars to support the mountain above. Nearly two centuries later, this same "room and pillar" method is still being used in the Khewra mine, which harvests some 400,000 tons of salt per year.

LITTLE BIG SALT

Many references in books and online claim that Khewra is the largest mine in the world, though I have no clue where this statistic comes from. While it is true that the salt range in which it sits has the largest deposit of highly pure salt in the world, even the highest estimates put production at 416,500 tons. Impressive as that may be, it pales in comparison to the huge industrial salt mines elsewhere. Industrial salt maker K+S pulls 6.5 million tons per year out of its Salar Grande de Tarapacá mine in Chile's Atacama Desert. Compass Minerals pulls 7.25 million tons of salt per year from the Sifto mine in Goderich, Canada.

Those are just the rock salt mines. The massive solution mine in Holland, Esco, can produce some 8 million tons a year by pumping water into salt deposits and then evaporating it off to make crystallized salt. Sea salt production can be equally vast. The largest of these operations is Guerrero Negro, owned by the Mexican government and Mitsubishi International Corporation. Guerrero Negro produces 7 million tons per year. Mitsubishi had plans to grow the operation even bigger, but protesters concerned about the impact of the operation on wildlife put a stop to that. So by comparison, Himalayan salt is small potatoes.

About eighty-five miles west of Khewra, along the Indus River, lies the Kalabagh salt mine. Here salt is also mined using the room and pillar method. Mining is primarily done by hand, and mules are often the vehicles of choice for carrying the salt to the surface. Kalabagh boasts thirteen different types of salt strata in the mine's Precambrian seams, each with its own crystal qualities, colors, and shades.

The Warcha salt mine is famous for its transparent salt crystals that average 98 percent pure sodium chloride. The salt is particularly suited for grinding into natural salts for cooking and for use at the table. The salt deposit dates to the

Precambrian Era. Warcha has been in operation since 1872; mining there is still done primarily by hand.

The Jatta mines delve into a salt deposit that dates from the Tertiary Period, 65 million to 2.6 million years ago, making it a young whippersnapper in comparison to the region's Precambrian mines. The salt is of a good quality, especially for lovers of salt lamps. The crystals can come in lackluster shades of white, light gray, and dark gray, but others can come in silvery blue and even deeper blue! Despite these unusual colors, the salt averages 98 percent pure sodium chloride.

At Bahadur Khel salt is being produced from eleven quarries and five mines. The deposit dates from the Tertiary Period and is made up of salt crystals ranging from light to dark gray, with some blues as well.

The Karak mines are comprised of three underground mines delving into deposits from the Tertiary Period. The salt is considered high grade and is sold ground up as table salt. The salt crystals are mainly white and gray to gray-blue.

Each of the country's mines produces distinctive salts, and each contains a variety of quality grades that vary depending on where in the seam the salt comes from. Khewra is Pakistan's big mine, but it is not necessarily the best source for salt destined to be cut into Himalayan salt blocks. One problem with Khewra in particular is that dynamite is used for the mining. This contributes to dangerous and difficult labor conditions for the miners, and it potentially adds trace amounts of explosive residue to the salt.

The mines where I source my salt for The Meadow are a trade secret. The ideal salt for salt blocks comes from very deep in the seam. Mining is done using a combination of hand labor and modern technology. The boulders of salt are loaded onto small rail cars and then transferred to big trucks using forklifts—about as hands-on as any mining anywhere in the world. The mines offer free medical care and employ experienced workers, primarily from local villages. In my opinion, it is important to buy your salt blocks from someone who can discern their quality and also vouch for the standards used to produce them.

SUSTAINABLE SALT BLOCKS

Are salt blocks sustainable? The short answer is yes: Practically, economically, and environmentally speaking, using salt blocks is not bad for the planet, and it is good for the planet's people.

Salt blocks are a natural resource, and all of Pakistan's salt mines contain vast supplies of salt. The country's largest single mine holds 6.7 billion tons by some estimates, of which 220 million tons are readily accessible. Calculating that a 9 by 9 by 2-inch salt block weighs about 14 pounds and roughly 50 percent of the raw salt gets cut away to be used in other salt products, the mine could theoretically produce enough salt to yield 18 billion salt blocks per year. At the current rate of mining, that could be sustained for another five centuries, and if expanded to access just 20 percent of the mine's total reserves, another three millennia. Since that's just one of a few dozen mines around the world that could produce salt blocks, practically speaking, we're not going to run out of salt blocks.

Can nature renew our salt block reserves? There are 1.3 billion cubic kilometers of water in the ocean, and each liter contains about 35 grams of salt. Converting that to imperial pounds, that pencils out to 1×10^{20} pounds—enough to bury all the landmass on earth with a 500-foot-deep drift of salt. We have plenty of salt to go around.

Unlike pollution from manufacturing and disposing of metals, plastics, and so forth, salt is a 100 percent natural product, and its interactions with the planet are neutral. Virtually all the salt we eat or cook with goes right back out of our bodies, returning to the sea from whence it came. Oceans continually shift, rise, sink, and occasionally evaporate into salt flats. In another few million years, the salt in your salt block, along with the salt in you, will be right back in the ocean, where it came from, no worse for the wear.

Economically speaking, the emerging market for salt blocks can only help the people where the blocks are produced. The raw salt mined in Pakistan is sold at commodity prices. People in the culinary sphere who advocate for recognizing salt as a natural, artisan food can do only so much to promote its valuation in global markets. It's not pretty, but there is a hard, low ceiling to the amount of money that a salt miner can make. Salt blocks, on the other hand, require very high-quality salt boulders, and only certain mines and certain mining practices can produce them. A premium price can and is put on the boulders, so miners can earn more money making them. In addition, unlike many products where raw materials are taken from the country of origin for a pittance and then transformed into value-added products elsewhere, salt blocks are mined, cut, packed, and transported domestically in Pakistan. Buyers such as myself pay 10 to 20 times more for this product than for the granular salt from these mines, and we're glad to do it. Also, all the leftover scrap is transformed into other salt products, so there is little waste.

No doubt mining salt blocks is hard work, but the best salt blocks are mined using the best practices. While workers at mines producing cheap Himalayan salt are exposed to the dangers of high explosives and their associated chemicals, it is possible to buy from mines that use no explosives. Skilled workers practice time-honored methods. These are the more desirable places to work, and those who work there defend their jobs.

Salt blocks give everyone involved in producing them a hand in creating something valuable and sustainable. Using salt blocks and sharing a meal on them can help support hard-working but economically disadvantaged people in a distant land.

Salt Block User Manual

The following guide provides practical information for procuring, using, caring for, and eventually recycling your salt block. If you are planning on heating up your salt block to cook on it, please refer to the important cautions on page 25 and Best Practices on page 109.

BLOCK SHOPPING

The better quality the salt block, the longer it will last and the less likely it is that something will go wrong, such as breaking or even exploding (see Caveat Clibano: Beware Your Oven, page 31). The best way to ensure quality is to buy your salt block from a trusted brand or from a dealer who has excellent, direct contacts at the source. My business, The Meadow, has a large selection of quality salt blocks available online or in New York and Portland, Oregon, or you can seek out a seller closer to home.

Pay a little extra; the best-quality salt costs more. There are many people producing salt blocks in Pakistan, but most of them deal in inferior grades of salt, either because it is far more economical or because they don't know any better. Ideally, buy from a retailer that provides guarantees against breakage. Avoid going for the cheapest block from an anonymous retailer who offers no written guarantee.

Before shopping, decide what you want to use your salt block for. Some vendors now differentiate the quality of the blocks according to their end use. At The Meadow we grade blocks as "tableware" for room temperature or cool uses as well as serving, "cookware" for heating, and "architectural" for construction of things like walls in spas and restaurants, light sculptures, and handmade meat lockers for dry aging.

Serving foods at room temperature or cooler requires no special structural qualities in the salt block. If you're serving, purchase your block for its beauty. I recommend choosing these salt blocks for their flaws rather than their homogeneous perfection. It's the fissures, deposits, varying translucency, and polychrome beauty that turns heads and makes the food really stand out. Choose a block in whatever dimension you wish (see Salt Block Sizing Guide, page 15), noting that thinner blocks often catch the light beautifully, while thicker pieces bring an imposing physical presence to the table.

A salt block destined for cooking is subject to more stringent requirements. The block will need to withstand the stresses of thermal expansion and contraction while heating and cooling. The block should be at least 1 inch thick, and preferably 1½ inches thick or more. My preference is to use 2-inch-thick blocks because they are stronger, hold heat longer, and look more imposing if I bring it to the table. For cooking, the physical beauty of the block is irrelevant because the block will change to an opaque, pale pink-white once it's heated. It will look pretty enough, but it will not have tableware's glowing, just-dropped-in-from-outer-space beauty.

THE SALT BLOCK CHEF'S DREAM SETUP

Cookware	9x9x2	4x8x2	Salt Bowl
Tableware	8x16x2	two 8x8x2	

For cooking, keep a 9x9x2 cookware on hand for regular use and a 4x8x2 brick for smashing things under a hot brick on the grill. In addition, two good oven mitts are essential for braving the fiery fun. For serving things when entertaining, use the biggest block you can get, either an 8x16x2 or a 9x18x2 serving platter. A modest 8x8x2 tableware block does the job preparing and serving cool, cold, and cured dishes. An additional 8x8x2 block can be used with the other 8x8x2 block to cure foods by sandwiching them between two blocks. A bowl is essential, if only for chocolate fondue, which you should be eating at least weekly.

Before heating.

After heating, a salt block's vibrant color will change. So a salt block can be used indefinitely for serving and then cooked on later, but it cannot be cooked on and then used for serving.

Pick your cooking block for its plainness. It should have minimal deep cracks, and any strata of color should be soft rather than clearly defined. Ideally, the block should be consistently translucent (not transparent), but opaque blocks can work well, too. Avoid any block that has lots of loose, "crunchy"-looking crystal facets throughout. These blocks can be the most beautiful for serving, but the facets harbor moisture. The moisture will vaporize when heated, causing the block to break or even pop like a giant piece of halite popcorn.

HAVE YOUR SALT BLOCK AND EAT IT, TOO

The best option is to buy at least two blocks, one for serving and one for cooking. If that simply isn't in the cards for you, keep in mind that using salt blocks is like dating. You can flirt around with cool and room temperature recipes for as long as you like, but once you go all the way (and cook on it, that is), there's no going back. The ancient youthful beauty of the block vanishes when you heat it. The block will turn paler, and it will develop tiny cracks and patina from the foods cooked on it.

In short, cooking on a block transforms it from a thing of beauty into a thing of practicality—but what practicality! You can use the same block for scallops one day and steak the next and duck breast the next and eggs after that. Unless the dish is something intensely oily and fragrant, like fresh sardines, the salt block will not carry over flavors of the preceding meal into the next.

Before cooking with a salt block for the first time, give it a quick cleaning. Salt is inherently sanitary (it is a natural disinfectant), but passing it briefly under cold water removes any dust or debris. Wipe with a clean cloth to dry. Paper towels work okay, but any rough bits on the surface of the block may catch and shred the paper, leaving a little confetti behind. Another benefit of rinsing the block is that it dissolves some of the bits of salt flaked up during manufacturing and transportation, burnishing it to its naturally lush, resonant color.

SALT BLOCK SIZING GUIDE

Base your purchase of a salt block on the types of foods you plan to use with it. The first consideration is whether you plan to serve on it or cook on it. The second is how large or heavy the block needs to be for the kind of recipes you will make. Larger and heavier salt blocks are generally more versatile, but with a little creativity even recipes calling for large platters can often be adapted to single portions served on small blocks. Note that the sizes specified in the recipes in this book are merely recommendations, and that it is generally possible to substitute multiple smaller blocks for a single larger one, or to prepare any given dish in multiple rounds on a single smaller block.

BLOCK SIZE	GRADE	RECIPES	PAGE
Thin and Small 4x4x¾ 5x5x1 4x8x¾ (recipes calling for large blocks may be adapted to individual serving sizes)	serving	Salt-Sloughed Butter (with Radishes, Brioche, and Fresh Peas)	50
	serving	A Capella Salt Block Antipasto	57
	serving	Salt and Pepper Semi-Cured Hamachi Sashimi	46
	serving	Salt Block Ceviche of Scallops, Snapper, and Shrimp	52
	serving	Smoked Salmon and Fresh Salmon Carpaccio Meet on a Salt Block Platter	54
	serving	Salt-Chopped Tenderloin Tartare with Quick-Cured Vegetable Pickles	41
	serving	Fleur de Salt Block Caramels	187
	serving	Watermelon and Feta on a Salt Block	45
	serving	Salted Peanut Brittle	184
	serving	Gold-Crusted Salty Chocolate Curls	190

BLOCK SIZE	GRADE	RECIPES	PAGE
Thick and Small 4x8x2 6x6x1½ 6 (round)x1½ 6 (round)x 2	cooking	Salt Brick Grilled Chicken	111
	serving	Salt-Sloughed Butter (with Radishes, Brioche, and Fresh Peas)	50
	serving	A Capella Salt Block Antipasto	57
	serving	Salt-Cured Candied Strawberries	70
	serving	Watermelon Ham and Melon	75
	cooking	Chèvre Brûlée and Arugula Wilted on Warm Salt with Pears	94
	cooking	Salt Block Smashed Potatoes	101
	serving	Chocolate-Covered Salt-Sopped Cherries	181
Thick and Large 8x8x1½ 8x8x2 9 (round)x1½ 9 (round)x 2 9x9x1½ 9x9x2	serving	Salt and Pepper Semi-Cured Hamachi Sashimi	46
	serving	Salt Block Ceviche of Scallops, Snapper, and Shrimp	52
	serving	Quick Salt Cod	65
	serving	Salt Block Cucumber Salad	69
	serving	Quick-Cured Vegetable Pickles	72
	serving	Sun-Dried Salt Block Tomatoes	78
	serving	Salt-Tanned Spiced Beef Leather	80
	serving	Preserved Savage Mushrooms	77
	serving	Salt Block Preserved Lemon Slices	82
	cooking	Molten Brie with Pistachio Crumbs and Warm Salted Dates	89
	cooking	Salt Block Raclette with Fire-Roasted New Potatoes and Shallots	102
	cooking	Salt Block Pressed Veal Paillard with Black Garlic Puree and Sage	116
	cooking	Salt Block Cheesesteaks	118
	cooking	Salt-Grilled Cheeseburger Sliders	121
	cooking	Salt Block Beef Fajitas	123
	cooking	Salt Block Seared Kobe Beef with Tarragon-Shallot Butter	126
	cooking	Salt-Grilled Peppered Pork Tenderloin	128
	cooking	Salt-Seared Calf's Liver and Bacon	130

BLOCK SIZE	GRADE	RECIPES	PAGE
Thick and Large 8x8x1½ 8x8x2 9 (round)x1½ 9 (round)x 2 9x9x1½ 9x9x2	cooking	Salt-Crisped Whole Fish with Mint and Pickled Ginger	131
	cooking	Salt Crust Scallops with Thai Lime Dipping Sauce	134
	cooking	Salt-Cooked Chanterelle Frittata	142
	cooking	Salt Block Rosemary Potato Chips	137
	cooking	Salt Block Asparagus Rolled in Pancetta with Mostarda Dipping Sauce	145
	cooking	Salt-Seared Sweet Potato Pancakes with Hot Pepper Honey	148
	cooking	Salt-Roasted Poultry Gizzards Seasoned with Pastrami Pepper	150
	cooking	Salt-Seared Pineapple Steaks with Curried Agave Drizzle	154
	cooking	Cinnamon Salt Plantains with Lemon-Espresso Syrup	156
	cooking	Salt-Baked Walnut Brioche Scones	152
	cooking	Salt Crust Cardamom Naan	158
	cooking	Salt-Griddled Blini with Sour Cream and Salt-Cured Candied Strawberries	161
	cooking	Salt-Baked Johnnycakes	144
	cooking	Salt-Baked Rustic Apple-Onion Tart with Blue Cheese	163
	serving	Salt-Frozen Parmesan Ice Cream with Tomato Marmalade and Basil Gremolata	174
	serving	Salted Bitters Ice Cream	176
	serving	Salt-Cured Strawberry Ice Cream	179
	serving	Salt-Frozen Mocha–Panna Cotta Gelato	173
	serving	Fleur de Salt Block Caramels	187

BLOCK SIZE	GRADE	RECIPES	PAGE
Very Large 8x12x1½ 8x12x2 10x10x1½ 10x10x2 8x16x1½ 8x16x2 9x18x1½ 9x18x2	serving	Smoked Salmon and Fresh Salmon Carpaccio Meet on a Salt Block Platter	54
	serving	Salt-Chopped Tenderloin Tartare with Quick-Cured Vegetable Pickles	41
	serving	Salt Block Cured Gravlax	66
	cooking	Salt-Grilled Peppered Pork Tenderloin	128
	cooking	Salt Block Rosemary Potato Chips	137
	cooking	Salt Crust Cardamom Naan	158
	cooking	Salt Block Baked Pretzel Rolls with Mustard Butter	166
	cooking	Salt-Baked Chocolate Chip–Oatmeal Whoppers	168
	serving	Watermelon and Feta on a Salt Block	45
	cooking	Salt-Roasted Poultry Gizzards Seasoned with Pastrami Pepper	150
	serving	Salted Peanut Brittle	184
	serving	Gold-Crusted Salty Chocolate Curls	190
Small Bowl	serving	Salad of Four Endives, Three Herbs, Two Fruits, and One Cheese Tossed in a Salt Bowl	48
Medium Bowl	cooking	Gorgonzola–Olive Oil Queso with Dipping Figs	87
	cooking	Bagna Cauda Warmed in a Salt Bowl, Served with Artichokes	98
	cooking	Salt-Melted Chocolate Fondue with Crisp Bacon	96
Large Bowl	serving	Salt Bowl Mayo and Variations: Aioli, Real Russian Dressing, and Sauce Fines Herbes	58
	cooking	Warm Black Bean Dip	91
Dish	cooking	Salt-Fried Molasses Duck Breast with Scallion Pancakes and Espresso Hoisin	113

BLOCK SIZE	GRADE	RECIPES	PAGE
Cup	serving	Quick-Cured Oyster with Gin Sangrita	199
	serving	Double-Fisted Tecate and Mezcal	198
	serving	Islay Scotch and Chocolate	196
	serving	Amaro Salato	204
	serving	Iced Pepper Vodka Shooter	200
	serving	Salacious Julep	203
	serving	Café Calva	209
	serving	Warm Sake Shot with Daikon	205
	serving	Xocolatl Xtabentún	206
Broken	n/a	Prawns Stir-Seared with Hot Aromatic Salt Rocks	139
	n/a	Fifteen Ways to Celebrate a Broken Salt Block	140

PAVE YOUR GRILL WITH SALT BLOCKS

Larger salt blocks can cook more and larger food. That said, don't assume you need to buy a huge platter just because you want to sauté primavera for ten people. I generally prefer to pave my grill with six to ten brick-size salt blocks rather than use one or two platter-size salt blocks.

One advantage to smaller blocks is that they are easier to handle and clean. Another advantage is that because they are smaller, they are less prone to breakage, and if they do break, you simply replace one of the small bricks the next time you're cooking, rather than go on the market for a whole new platter. You can always keep using a broken platter, but if it is going to break there is often no telling how it will break, and you could be left with one or more pieces that are too small or irregularly shaped to use. Also, the larger salt blocks and platters often cost considerably more than the equivalent surface area made up of smaller salt blocks.

The other advantage to paving is the increased flexibility. When you have many brick-size blocks, you can custom pave the area of your grill according to the needs of each meal. Sometimes I'll pave just a corner of the grill and light the fire under the block side of the grill only. Then I can sear some chicken on the salt block and finish it on the exposed grill grate, where it cooks indirectly from the convection currents trapped under the hood of the grill. Other times, such as at a big barbecue, I'll pave the entire grill from end to end and sear up a mess of shrimp and skirt steak.

Paving isn't perfect, of course. You do have to be cognizant of the cracks between blocks when putting food on them, but I find that the advantages often outweigh the inconvenience.

BAKE WITH SALT PIZZA STONES

Salt blocks make fantastic pizza stones. A pizza stone emulates the effect of a commercial pizza oven in the home. Usually made of flat stone or heavy ceramic, the pizza stone's surface absorbs some of the moisture of the dough to produce a crispy crust. In addition, it distributes heat evenly, contributes thermal mass, and transfers heat rapidly to ensure that the pizza or baked goods cook properly.

Put your tempered salt block (see page 30) in the cold oven and allow it to warm up with the oven to the desired temperature, and allow an additional 15 minutes for the salt block to heat fully. Several smaller salt blocks on a sheet pan can also be used. If cooking at the proper temperature, the heat of the salt stone will usually cook the pizza dough so quickly that it doesn't stick to the salt blocks at all, yet the initial contact imbues the dough with a fine crispy saltiness. Concerns about sticking can be allayed by sprinkling the hot salt block with a little cornmeal or semolina just before adding the pizza.

UTENSILS AND GEAR

There are not many places in the world you'll find an encomium on oven mitts, but it's warranted here. Heavy, professional-grade oven or grill mitts are indispensible for cooking food on salt blocks. A big salt block on a barbecue grill or stovetop is bulky, awkward, very heavy, and potentially very, very hot. It is often necessary to put hands right over the fire when positioning a block or holding it in place to flip or remove food. Salt blocks don't have handles, so moving one from a grill or stove means lifting it from the bottom, right where the fire was heating it. Those cute oven mitts crocheted back at summer camp are not going to cut it. Use only professional-grade oven mitts that provide the following: (1) solid protection against high heat for at least 1 minute; (2) resistance to temperatures up to at least 800°F; (3) flame retardation (especially if lifting the block from a lit grill); and (4) good grip. Standard consumer oven mitts will not be up to this task. Silicone mitts melt at around 500°F, and cotton and wool ones burn or singe at around 600°F. My preference is for puppet-style mitts with Kevlar palms and thumbs and fire-retardant Nomex uppers and sleeves. They're not the cheapest—a pair will run about $75, but a trip to the emergency room will run about $1,500. Get professional oven mitts from hospitality industry suppliers

like San Jamar and M. Tucker. You can show them off to your friends in public and marvel at your unblemished hands in private.

A good stainless-steel spatula is the essential implement for sautéing on a salt block. Salt is not a nonstick surface, so food will cling to it. Turning or removing the food with a rubber, wood, or Teflon spatula will likely leave that most beautiful of beautiful food layers, that beautifully browned and salted sliver of heaven, on the block. To flip or remove food, hold the salt block steady with a thick oven mitt or grill mitt, and then press down very firmly, scraping hard along the surface of the salt block. Don't be afraid to put some muscle into it!

Salt bowls with a small base may not fit squarely on the burner grate of a stovetop. The last thing anyone needs after a delicious, relaxing meal is fondue spilled all over the stove. Find a small steel cooling rack or any small cross-hatched grate that can fit over the burner to give the bowl a stable foundation upon which to sit.

For foods prepared on room temperature or warm salt blocks, no special tools are needed. A small silicone rubber spatula is handy for stirring foods in salt bowls. The more you stir, the more salt the food takes on, faster; so in a way the spatula is the tool for seasoning. If your bean dip or bagna cauda needs a little salt, a swirl with the spatula will stir in a little additional salt from the edges where the food has already dissolved some of the salt. A small spatula also serves very well for stirring and tidying up the bowl when making chocolate fondue.

Trivets are another essential for cooking on or serving from hot salt blocks at the table. Ceramic is an excellent insulator and can withstand very high temperatures. Do not use trivets of silicone or wood, as they will melt or burn, ruining your salt block or your trivet, or both. Whatever you do, do not use a metal trivet. Metal will resist the heat just fine, but it will also conduct all that energy from the salt block right to your table! This will almost certainly ruin your table—not to mention the real tragedy that it will also drain heat from the block so rapidly that it will not do its job cooking the food. The ideal materials are highly heat-resistant materials with low thermal conductivity, such as ceramic.

My preferred setup is a solid ceramic trivet with a silicone trivet beneath that to provide added thermal insulation and resistance to slippage.

Infrared laser thermometers can be helpful for gauging the temperature of salt blocks. These are little gun-shaped lasers that you aim at a nonreflective surface; pull the trigger and you get an accurate temperature reading. Once very expensive, laser thermometers are now quite affordable. A laser thermometer should be rated to measure up to 700°F. Some also measure cool temperatures to –50°F or lower. Most cooks can also get a pretty good sense of the temperature of a salt block by spattering a little water on it and observing how rapidly it evaporates (see Getting It Hot, page 24).

A portable propane burner is a very handy appliance that lets you cook whole meals on a salt block right at the table (see Handling below).

HANDLING

Hot: Salt blocks heat to well in excess of 600°F, and the bottom of the block may be much hotter than the top, so treat them with the same precautions you would any hot pan. However, unlike a skillet, salt blocks don't have handles. Always use very heavy, fire-resistant oven mitts when handling your salt block. I use a pair of commercial-grade Kevlar and Nomex oven mitts I purchased at a restaurant supply store (see Utensils and Gear, page 21).

Note that salt blocks hold more than ten times as much energy as a pot, so anything you set them on after removing them from the fire will be subject to intense heat. A hot block can easily scorch your table, your counter, or you. Before moving a hot salt block, prepare a place to put it such as a trivet (see Utensils and Gear, page 21) or a spot on your range, turn off the heat source (if possible) to reduce the risk of scorching your oven mitts, and alert others around you that you are coming through with a hot salt block in your hands.

Another option is to do all the cooking at the table. While the heated salt block will stay hot enough for one, two, and even possibly three rounds of thinly sliced flank steak, it will nonetheless cool rapidly enough that it will affect the

flavor of your food. The cooler block will require the food to cook longer, which will give the food more time to release moisture and pick up more salt. By round three or four, your flank steak will be pretty salty. For meals where you want to cook for extended periods of time, use a portable propane burner. You can buy these inexpensively at a restaurant supply or camping store.

Cool: When using a salt block to serve food at the table, be sure to set it on a protective trivet, plate, or cutting board to keep your table from being scratched by the heavy stone of salt. Otherwise, handle your salt block like you would any other piece of kitchenware.

Frozen: Always use oven mitts when handling a frozen salt block. I say this for practical as well as aesthetic reasons. Your hands are warm, so they will warm the block up unnecessarily every time you touch it. Also, your warm hands will leave marks where they have melted the frosty surface of the block. Wearing oven mitts and gently handling the block from the bottom preserves its bristling frozen beauty.

GETTING IT HOT

A salt block's warmup rate depends on the amount of energy put into it and the mass of the block. Before heating your salt block for the first time, please refer to Read Before Heating! (page 25) for important cautions and disclaimers.

Larger blocks take longer to heat than smaller ones, and weaker heat sources need more time to heat a block than more powerful ones. In addition, there are some basic physics to consider.

A nice expensive 10-inch aluminum-core stainless-steel frying pan weighs about 2½ pounds and has about 200 square inches of surface area with the rim. A 10-inch diameter, 1½-inch-thick salt block has about the same surface area, but it weighs 12 pounds. This mass takes energy and time to heat, and to cool.

READ BEFORE HEATING!

A salt block ain't a factory-fresh steel skillet. It is a natural stone from time out of mind. It requires special treatment. Heed the following when heating a salt block.

- Salt blocks can crack. Heat them slowly.
- Salt blocks can pop. Only use cookware-graded blocks.
- Salt blocks get very hot. Handle them only very briefly, using extreme caution, wearing professional high-temperature oven mitts (see Utensils and Gear, page 21).
- Salt blocks hold enormous energy. Ensure there is adequate insulation between salt blocks and tables or counters.
- Disclaimer: Cooking on salt blocks poses risks. If you wish to cook on one, please understand that you assume all responsibility. Neither I nor my publisher is responsible for any damages, injury, or loss related to the use of Himalayan salt products.
- Follow Best Practices provided on page 109.

In addition, every pound of salt stores 2 kilojoules of energy versus well under 1 kilojoule of energy stored by the pan. The pan heats and cools rapidly because it only holds a small amount of energy, and because the aluminum in it conducts heat incredibly well. The salt block can contain approximately 10 times the amount of energy. On top of that, the salt is not very conductive, so energy is slow to travel through it.

Most of the time you will start heating the block before you even begin assembling ingredients for your dish. Place the salt block over a burner on your stove and set it to its lowest possible setting for 15 minutes. Giving your salt block at least 15 minutes to warm up from room temperature to 150°F or 200°F allows it to evaporate off any moisture locked in the matrix of the crystals, and allows

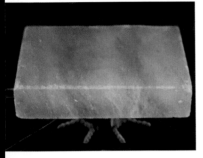

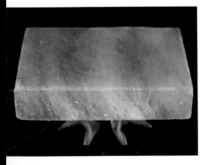

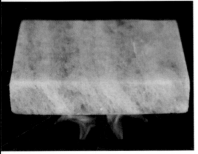

Stages of heating cold to hot

the heat to spread evenly through the block, minimizing the stresses caused by expansion. This is especially important the first time you heat your salt block, or if you live in a humid environment and haven't used your salt block in a few months, as the salt block will continuously draw moisture from the atmosphere.

Patience is essential, and the process is so different from preheating an oven, a skillet, or a pot of pasta water that you need to adopt the habit of using a clock or timer to keep track, at least until you get the hang of it. The golden rule for heating blocks is "go slow," heating salt blocks in 15-minute stages. This reduces the stresses caused from thermal expansion, minimizing the risk of breakage and prolonging the life of the block. How many stages depends on the temperature that needs to be achieved. Heating to 100°F to 200°F degrees can be achieved in one stage: very low. Heating a block to 550°F necessitates heating in three stages: stage 1, very low; stage 2, medium; and stage 3, high. The maximum temperature a salt block will achieve on most residential gas ranges is about 550°F.

While it is impossible to control precisely, the 35/55/55 guideline is a handy way to gauge where your salt block is on the road to reaching its desired temperature. During the first stage, with the stove on the lowest setting, the top surface of the salt block should increase in temperature from 35°F to 40°F every 5 minutes for 15 minutes. Fifteen minutes later, turning the heat to medium should increase the rate at which the block heats to 55°F every 5 minutes for 15 minutes total during the second stage. Turning the heat to high for the final stage may result in the block heating at the slightly slower rate of 45°F to 55°F as the power of the stove may start to max out. The 35/55/55 guideline applies to any method of direct heating, whether on a stove or a grill. Electric stoves may heat more slowly, so be prepared to add 5 minutes to each 15-minute stage.

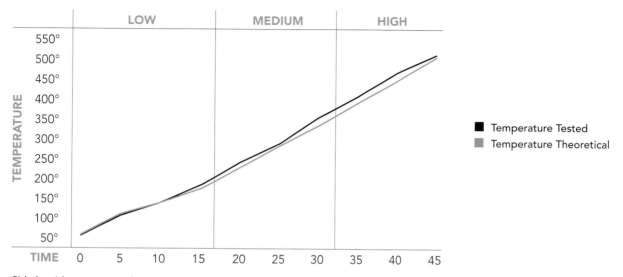

Side-by-side comparison between heating an actual 8 by 8 by 2-inch salt block on a home gas range, and the results that should theoretically be achieved by following the guidelines of heating a salt block in three stages and aiming for 35/55/55 degrees every 5 minutes.

The following chart provides a guideline for heating blocks to anywhere from 100°F to over 500°F. Note that larger salt blocks will take longer to heat than smaller ones, so this is only a guideline. Also note that in general it is better to cook with a salt block that is too hot rather than one that is not hot enough, achieving a bold salt sear rather than a slow salt simmer (see Best Practices on page 109).

	STAGE 1	STAGE 2	STAGE 3
Heating to Very Low (100°F to 175°F)	5 min.		
Heating to Low (175°F to 250°F)	10 min.		
Heating to Medium-Low (250°F to 300°F)	15 min.		
Heating to Medium (300°F to 400°F)	15 min.	15 min.	
Heating to Medium-High (400°F to 450°F)	15 min.	15 min.	10 min.
Heating to High (500°F +)	15 min.	15 min.	15+ min.

Preheating

Slow preheating is especially important the first time you use your salt block because it is the most stressful time for the block. Because the salt block is very thick, different parts of the block are at different temperatures while it heats, and different rates of thermal expansion put stress on the block. In addition, the different mineral components, various crystalline structures, and any existing cracks each react differently as the temperature rises from room temperature to several hundred degrees. There may also be small amounts of moisture within the salt itself, accumulated along the road from the womb of the mountains in Pakistan to your kitchen counter. Heating the salt block very slowly the first time gives the crystals an opportunity to form the microfissures that lend a little extra elasticity to the block, and it also gives any moisture time to escape. This extra care during first-time use greatly will extend your block's lifespan.

Gas Stove

On a gas stove, increase the heat in increments every 15 minutes, from low to medium and from medium to high. Depending on the size of the block, it should take 40 to 50 minutes to heat a block from room temperature to its high temperature of 500°F to 550°F. Infrared laser thermometers are a great tool for gauging the precise temperature of a salt block (see Utensils and Gear, page 21), but anyone familiar with heating a skillet will get the hang of it pretty quickly. A rough estimate of temperature can be gleaned by spattering water on the surface: At 300°F, the water will boil off in 2 to 5 seconds; at 400°F it will sizzle off in 1 to 2 seconds; and at 500°F it will hardly touch the surface before skating off and vanishing in its own vapor.

Electric Stove

On an electric stove, use a ½- to 1-inch metal ring such as a sturdy pastry ring to keep the block away from direct contact with the heating element. A stainless-steel, pop-out bottom tart pan with the bottom popped out is perfect. Heat diffusers are not recommended as they can create hotspots on the salt block that would stress it and cause it to crack. Raise the heat in gradual increments, every 15 to 20 minutes, allowing at least 45 minutes total to heat the block.

Gas Grill

Gas grills are an excellent way to heat the blocks. Put the block on the grill directly over one of the burners, put the top down, and turn the burner to low. After 15 minutes, fire up another burner and turn both to medium, increasing the heat in increments similarly to the way you would on a gas stove.

Charcoal Grill

When warming salt blocks on a charcoal grill, set up your grill for bilevel medium heat (about 325°F on the grill hood's thermometer). This means making two levels of coals: one about four coals in depth and one no more than one coal deep. Heat the salt block directly on the grill grate over low heat for 15 minutes. Then move the block halfway between the high- and low-heat areas and heat for another 15 minutes. Move the salt block over to the high-heat area and heat for 15 minutes more.

GAUGING TEMPERATURE

After you have cooked on your salt block a few times, you will get a sense of where the salt block is in the heating process just by looking at it and holding your hand over it to sense its warmth. A great way to tell if a salt block is 500°F to 525°F (the best all-around temperature for searing most foods) is to slowly move your hand toward the surface of the hot salt block. If your hand stops about 1½ inches away and says, "No way, Jose," that's 500°F to 525°F. My state-of-the-art infrared laser thermometer is forgotten in a drawer because I actually get better results gauging temperatures with my hands.

TIP: WIND DOWN THE HEAT

Turn off the heat or remove the salt block from the hot grill a few minutes before the food is done cooking. The block will continue to cook the food for some minutes at virtually the same temperature as the energy from the bottom of the block continues to conduct through to the top, so cooking will not be affected. The advantage is that the block will start cooling down just enough so that when the food is removed, it will have much less energy with which to carbonize any food left adhering to the block. Not only will this make the block much easier to clean but it will also help preserve its natural good looks by reducing the patina that comes from too much burned-on food.

On a related note, turning the heat to low for two to three minutes before turning it completely off slows down the rate of cooling, minimizing the thermal stresses. While I have never had a problem with a block breaking due to its cooling too fast, there is an audible difference in the amount of crackling sounds coming from the block when this method is used, indicating that the crystals are experiencing less stress.

Oven

The most bulletproof way to heat a salt bock for use in the oven is to preheat it on the stovetop first, while the oven is preheating, and then transfer the hot block to the hot oven. Heat the block as described on page 28 until it reaches at least 300°F (for use as a pizza stone, the block can be heated well in excess of 500°F, as desired).

If you bake or roast a lot, preheating blocks and transferring them to the oven may be an onerous process. Tempering the block in advance can make using them in the oven much more convenient. The first time you use a salt block, heat it to about 400°F on a stovetop as previously described. Maintain at this temperature for 30 minutes. This will rid it of any trapped moisture, and it will then be safe to use in an oven environment. The block can then be put in the hot oven for immediate use, or allowed to cool for use later. It is not necessary to re-temper a block that is being heated frequently, but if it sits in humid air for more than a month without being heated, it should be tempered again before oven use. (Some salt block vendors claim to make their salt blocks oven safe by tempering them before selling them. But these salt blocks will draw right back in all the moisture they originally lost.) For many people the best way to use a block in the oven will be to simply preheat it on the stove and then transfer it to the hot oven.

CAVEAT CLIBANO: BEWARE YOUR OVEN

Disregard any sources you might come across that advise heating salt blocks in the oven. It is possible, but it is not the ideal way to go about it. Ovens are humid environments. Gas ovens are particularly humid environments. They burn natural gas, which is methane (CH_4). When methane burns, each CH_4 molecule combines with two O_2 molecules to make one CO_2 and two H_2O molecules. In other words, for every molecule of methane you burn, you get two of water. So, implausible as it seems, 1 pound of methane yields 2.25 pounds of water. A typical commercial convection oven burns about 2 pounds of fuel an hour, producing 9 pounds or more than 1 gallon of water!

Consider the wisdom of heating a salt block in a water factory. Salt blocks are hygroscopic, meaning they love to draw moisture out of the air. Imagine putting a cool, hygroscopic block into a warm, humid oven. The humidity immediately condenses onto the salt block. Now you have a cool, wet block in a warm oven. As the block warms, the water evaporates off, and as with real perspiration on your body, this cools the block even more. Now you have a lot of thermal stresses competing within your block. The result can be, quite literally, explosive, resulting in severe damage to your oven and even injury to anyone nearby. I know of many dozens, if not hundreds, of exploded salt blocks, broken oven doors, and shattered nerves.

You can use your oven as the primary way to heat salt blocks, but it is not advised unless absolutely necessary. For professional chefs who need to keep large numbers of salt blocks very hot and at the ready, oven heating may be your best or your only option. If this is the case, again beware that you may occasionally have a salt block explode in your oven (especially the first time a block is heated), but this risk can be greatly reduced by following a few basic rules.

First, only buy cookware-grade blocks that are free of the grainy crystal compositions that harbor moisture. Cheap, loosely grained salt blocks are not only far more prone to popping, but they are also somewhat prone to breaking, which could spell a service disaster. Cookware-grade blocks virtually never break unexpectedly.

Second, don't heat your salt blocks in the water factory that is a gas oven. If you are going to heat salt blocks in an oven, use an electric convection oven if at all possible.

Third, as always, heat your salt blocks slowly, especially the first time. Put the salt block in the cold oven and set to 250°F for 20 to 30 minutes. Next, bump up the heat to 350°F for 15 minutes, and then up to the desired final temperature and allow at least 15 minutes before using. A good trick is to put a dozen or more salt blocks in the oven at one time. This slows the heating process and gives the blocks ample time to gently expand and lose any moisture locked in them. Add 5 to 15 minutes per stage if heating multiple bocks. Once hot, the salt block can be kept in the oven indefinitely.

GETTING IT COLD

Just as it takes more time to make ice cubes than it does to boil water, it takes even longer to cool a salt block than to heat it. It makes sense if you think about it. A typical stove burner directs about 7,000 Btu at the block, which is about twice the amount of energy that even a very powerful home freezer can take out.

A refrigerator will cool a block down to 35°F to 38°F. Allow a minimum of an hour for small blocks that are less than 1 inch thick. Thicker blocks will require at least a few hours.

A freezer will cool a block to 0°F. (Technically, since the block is already a solid, you are not freezing the block at all but simply cooling it to below the freezing point of water.) A small block will take two to three hours to reach temperature. Allow all day or overnight for large blocks. There is no sure-fire way to tell if a salt block is frozen by looking at it (except that in warm, humid atmospheres, they do often frost up when removed from the freezer), so either use an infrared thermometer that is capable of reading cold temperatures or just allow the allotted time for them to chill completely. Because a frozen block will keep a steady temperature, it doesn't matter how long the block remains in the freezer after reaching 0°F. For that reason, it is probably easiest to put a block to be used for freezing in the freezer the day before it is needed.

CLEANING

Allow the block to cool fully to room temperature before washing, at least three or four hours. Moisten the salt block by wiping it with a wet sponge, then scrub vigorously at any areas where food has stuck with a steel scouring pad (a green scrubby will also work), and wipe away any loosened pieces with a damp sponge. Do not use a soap-infused pad like SOS or Brillo, as the soap may penetrate the block and ruin it. Repeat the process until the surface is clean, then pat dry with a clean rag or paper towels. Allow to sit out for a few hours more to evaporate off any remaining moisture.

Note that no salt block will ever return to its original unused state of splendor. It will turn an opaque, pale white-pink. It is okay to clean off any adhering food, but don't obsess on scrubbing it all the way down to a pristine state. Like a cast-iron skillet, salt blocks should take on a natural patina from the foods cooked on them. Excessive cleaning will shorten the life of the block.

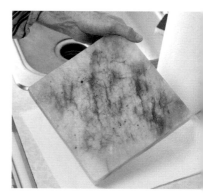

STORAGE

Note: Salt blocks are hygroscopic (water-attracting). They will suck moisture right out of the air, but unless you live in the 99 percent humidity of a Borneo jungle, you can probably leave your salt block on the counter or in a cupboard alongside other dishes. Store the block in a place where humidity is at a minimum. For most people, a countertop or cupboard in the kitchen or dining room is sufficient. Even though I live in the wet and rainy climes of the Pacific Northwest, my salt blocks do just fine scattered around the house wherever I happen to find a place for them.

If you do live in a humid place and your salt block is always damp (and maybe even tends to pool up water!), you can wrap it in a few layers of paper towels and seal it in a zipper-lock plastic bag to keep it from absorbing atmospheric moisture. Some people choose to keep their salt blocks in the refrigerator, where humidity is consistently low due to the simple fact that cold air holds less moisture than warm air. This does work okay, and makes it so you always have a chilled salt block at the ready, but it does take up valuable refrigerator space.

My favorite place to keep the beautiful salt blocks that I use frequently for serving purposes is on a windowsill, where they capture light and warm the room. Do not store your block near an oven, stove, or heater, where temperature and humidity fluctuate widely. Definitely do not store it outdoors.

DEATH OF A SALT BLOCK

How do you know if your salt block is kaput? Old salt blocks don't die; they just crumble away. A serving block may survive many hundreds of uses, and a well-maintained high-quality cookware block may last for dozens of uses, but salt blocks do eventually break. When they do, feel free to keep using them anyway. So long as the block presents a useful surface, you can continue to serve or cook with it.

The end of a block's utility as a block spells the beginning of its utility as a salt (see Fifteen Ways to Celebrate a Broken Salt Block, page 140). It is still

natural, good salt. Even blocks that have been cooked on extensively can still be used broken up and tossed into a skillet for a hot bed for cooking meats, fish, or root vegetables.

The Land That Time Remembered

Salt blocks are a gemstone-like mineral that also happens to be a food. This food wasn't produced a few days ago like your fresh produce, or a month ago like your aged meat, or a year ago like that awesome hard cheese you love, or even twenty-five years ago like the bottle of wine you fantasize about buying. This food "grew up" back when the planet was still a reckless youth, slamming into cataclysmic meteors with abandon, heaving 10,000-foot-tall waves of molten lava from vast fissures across its surface, and only just wrapping up with the slow gestation of the land, oceans, atmosphere, and biosphere we recognize today.

And if that wasn't enough to make you think twice, it now turns out that it is a food we can cook on. Perhaps for this reason it's taken until now for someone to write a book on the subject. But just because something is overlooked doesn't mean it isn't essential, arresting, and rewarding.

It has been 500 million years since the sun last warmed this salt as it collected on the shores of a primordial sea. Now it fairly hums with ancient luminescence on your kitchen counter. Listen to it. Of what discoveries does it whisper?

The recipes that follow are broken down into chapters, each one on the major techniques for preparing food on salt blocks. Any given chapter may contain recipes for entrées, main courses, sides, and condiments.

Chapter 1 kicks off with serving food on salt blocks at room temperature, with recipes that revel in the stunning visual impact of presenting food on a 600-million-year-old salt block and that also reveal how food and salt interact when left to their own devices. Chapter 2 delves into the craft of transforming the very nature of food, with recipes for curing with salt blocks to enhance flavor, improve texture, and, of course, preserve. Chapter 3 just loves a salt block for its body, taking advantage of its capacity for giving off warmth to create dishes that luxuriate in the heightened flavor and succulence that comes when fats begin to melt and aromas amplify. Chapter 4 puts the forces of heat to work—from the caramelization of sugars and carbohydrates to the Maillard reaction (browning of protein) to the subtler influences of the evaporation of moisture—while the salt block casts its own spells on the flavor and texture of food. Chapter 5 plunges into the subzero realm, using the physical bulk of the salt to freeze food into deliciousness. Chapter 6 offers solutions for having fun cooking, entertaining, and dining with cocktails that can be sipped straight from the salt lip of cups milled from a salt rock.

THE SIRENS OF SALT BLOCK SALTINESS

Salt blocks see it as their elemental duty to bring the brio and bounce to your food. It is your job to harness nature's will and bend it to your own. Master the five basic physical principles behind cooking on salt blocks and you will get great results every time.

- MOISTURE: Wetter foods take on more salt faster.
- TIME: The longer a food cooks on a salt block, the more salt it absorbs.
- TEMPERATURE: Searing food on a very hot salt block reduces the amount of salt it absorbs.
- FAT: Fat on a salt block reduces the amount of salt interacting with the surface of the food.
- THICKNESS: Thick and dense food can interact longer with a salt block surface without becoming too salty.

CHAPTER 1

SERVING ON SALT BLOCKS

Salt-Chopped Tenderloin Tartare with
Quick-Cured Vegetable Pickles

Watermelon and Feta on a Salt Block

Salt and Pepper Semi-Cured Hamachi Sashimi

Salad of Four Endives, Three Herbs, Two Fruits,
and One Cheese Tossed in a Salt Bowl

Salt-Sloughed Butter (with Radishes, Brioche, and Fresh Peas)

Salt Block Ceviche of Scallops, Snapper, and Shrimp

Smoked Salmon and Fresh Salmon Carpaccio
Meet on a Salt Block Platter

A Capella Salt Block Antipasto

Salt Bowl Mayo and Variations: Aioli,
Real Russian Dressing, and Sauce Fines Herbes

Salt blocks are both beautiful and precious, which makes them more than just a mineral; it makes them a gem—a gem that captures empyrean light and binds it, transforming photons into a radiant, translucent geometry. But unlike most gems, precious and precise, salt blocks are enormous cracked slabs of ore from the heart of the earth's 4-billion-year-old crust.

Serving food on a salt block is the simplest and one of the best ways to take advantage of its geological companionship. Use it as you would a platter or cutting board whenever you are dishing up foods that are servable at room temperature and would benefit from a little salt: fruits, cheeses, pâtés, fresh or steamed vegetables, and cured meats. A salt block imparts measured seasoning that increases in proportion to the moisture content of the food and the length of time it is on the block.

Butter will never get more than a glimmer of salt. At my house I set a stick of butter on a salt block at the breakfast table and leave it there. Keeping butter out of the fridge makes getting to it more convenient. Soft butter tastes better and is easier to use, and it looks more tantalizing. The salt prohibits bacterial growth, so the butter will stay fresh-tasting for days.

High-moisture ingredients, like watermelon, interact with the salt block more overtly, giving you a short window during which the seasoning goes from delicate to flat-out intense. What starts out as a delicately salted snack after five minutes will transform into a quick pickle within a half hour.

Beyond these recipes specifically created to serve on salt blocks, many other recipes can be adapted to serve on salt blocks to stunning effect. Put your salt block on the stovetop set to low and warm it for 15 minutes slightly. Then use the salt block as a serving platter for all your cooked meats, from burgers to pork chops. The platter adds a little last-minute seasoning and also keeps things warm! The block can be set on a tray to catch any juices released from the meats. Use the same technique for serving rice, roasted winter roots, mashed potatoes, collard greens, grilled summer squash, artichokes, or buttery slices of garlic bread.

For some foods, especially shellfish, salting before cooking will toughen them up. Cook calamari, octopus, and shrimp without salt and serve them on a warm salt block to let their juices draw up salt when they need it: right before they go in your mouth. The last courses of the meal also love a little smooch of salt from a salt block, from cheeses and fruits to cakes. Place a full bar of dark chocolate on a warm salt block, let stand for 10 minutes, and then dip pretzels, fruit, or your fingers into the lusciously melted chocolate.

You deserve pleasure and beauty as part of your routine, not just for special occasions. Serving, preparing, and storing your food on a salt block is a tasty way to bring this lovely edible gemstone into your daily life.

Salt-Chopped Tenderloin Tartare with Quick-Cured Vegetable Pickles

The only thing separating the wolf's lust for raw meat from ours is seasoning and setting. Where wolves devour their meat on the frozen tundra, straight from the ribs of their kill, we nibble ours with salt and minced onions in the guise of well-heeled businessmen dining in global capitals. Serving tartare on a chilled salt block gives us some of the Arctic's cerulean vitality while salting with howling sophistication.

1 (8 by 12 by 2-inch or 10 by 10 by 2-inch) salt block platter

12 ounces well-trimmed lean beef tenderloin

2 teaspoons Worcestershire sauce

1 tablespoon Dijon mustard

1 egg yolk

2 anchovy fillets, finely chopped

10 capers, finely chopped

¼-inch-thick slice red onion, finely chopped

3 medium fresh chives, thinly sliced

2 teaspoons extra-virgin olive oil (the best you can afford)

1 big pinch finely crafted flaked salt, such as Halen Môn Silver

Freshly cracked black pepper

6 slices bread of your choice

2 cups Quick-Cured Vegetable Pickles (page 72), using your choice of vegetable

MAKES 4 SERVINGS

Refrigerate the salt block platter for at least 2 hours.

Slice the tenderloin into ⅛-inch-thick slices using the chilled salt block as a cutting board. Cut the slices into strips and the strips in small pieces. Chop until the meat is fine enough to mold but is still in separate pieces. Mix in the Worcestershire sauce, mustard, and egg yolk until well blended. Form into a disk about 6 inches across in the center of the salt block platter.

Mix the anchovies, capers, red onion, and chives together and scatter over the disk of tartare. Drizzle with the olive oil and season with the flaked salt and pepper to taste.

Toast the bread slices and cut them into quarters. Surround the tartare with the pickles and warm toasts and serve immediately. The recipe is designed to be casually eaten family style, but a more elegant presentation can be achieved by serving individual portions on smaller salt blocks.

Watermelon and Feta
on a Salt Block

Sprinkle some salt on a slice of watermelon and its flesh contracts to subtle firmness, its aroma blooms, and its flavor crescendos. If that's what a few scattered crystals can achieve, imagine what lavishing that slice with the unerring saline expanse of a salt block will do to it: fragrant, sensual, symphonic.

1 (8 by 12 by 2-inch) salt block platter, or 2 smaller blocks

4 (½-inch-thick) quarter slices large watermelon, rinds removed, or 8 (½-inch-thick) quarter slices small watermelon

3 ounces feta, crumbled

6 fresh mint leaves, slivered

MAKES 2 SERVINGS

Chill the salt block platter in the refrigerator for at least 2 hours.

Arrange the melon slices on the block, slightly overlapping—the more the overlap, the less salt imparted to the melon. Scatter the feta and mint leaves over the top. Serve immediately. For added pop, allow the dish to stand 20 minutes before serving.

Salt and Pepper Semi-Cured Hamachi Sashimi

A cut of fish glistening from the sea asks that we honor it. Simple slices of pristine hamachi can't bear the insult of ornamentation, but they are exalted by salt. Resting fresh fish flesh on a chilled block of salt returns it momentarily to its birthplace, impregnating it with salinity, firming its muscularity. You will need very high-quality fish for this dish. If you have access to an Asian market, the fishmonger there can usually get you sushi-grade hamachi. Plan ahead, because it might have to be special-ordered. Yes, I know it is pricey, but ecstasy isn't cheap.

1 (9-inch) square or round salt block

1 pound sushi-grade yellowtail
   flounder (hamachi)

2 Tellicherry peppercorns

4 dried green peppercorns

4 Szechuan peppercorns

⅛ teaspoon Aleppo pepper

2 scallions, roots and dark green ends
   trimmed, thinly sliced

4 thin lime slices

MAKES 4 SERVINGS

Chill the salt block in the refrigerator for at least 2 hours.

Cut the yellowtail into ½-inch-thick slices. Place the fish slices on the chilled salt block and refrigerate for 10 minutes. Then flip the pieces of fish so the other side comes in contact with the salt and refrigerate for another 5 minutes.

While the fish is curing, smash the Tellicherry, green, and Szechuan peppercorns with the flat side of a large knife, a meat pounder, or the bottom of a heavy skillet. Mix the peppercorns together with the Aleppo pepper.

To serve, scatter the pepper and scallions over the fish, and serve on the salt block with the lime slices. Squeeze a lime over the dish if desired, or save it for a salty lime dessert.

Salad of Four Endives, Three Herbs, Two Fruits, and One Cheese Tossed in a Salt Bowl

There's the thrill and romance of an ambitious salad plated beautifully by a rock star chef at a hip restaurant. There's the charm and comfort of a simple salad served family-style at home. At the former you are a tourist, gawking at the scenery. At the latter you are a king, but of a modest domain. Then there's the salad that brings out your own inner chef, that introduces a delicious salty setting to a chorus of bitter greens and fragrant herbs, that combines sweet fruit notes with savory blue creaminess, that is served to close friends by your own hand in the most enigmatically beautiful bowl ever to grace a dining table. Now you are an exotic wayfarer sharing a personal odyssey, like a treasure, resplendent.

4 (1- to 2-cup) salt bowls or small plates

2 tablespoons red wine vinegar

2 tablespoons extra-virgin olive oil

1 small garlic clove, minced

Freshly ground black pepper

1 small head radicchio, cored and torn into bite-size pieces

2 Belgian endives, cored and cut into tiny bite-size pieces

½ head escarole, cored and torn into bite-size pieces

½ head chicory, cored and torn into bite-size pieces

¼ cup packed fresh basil leaves

¼ cup packed fresh flat-leaf parsley

2 tablespoons chopped fresh chives

¼ cup pomegranate seeds (arils)

2 ounces blue cheese, crumbled

1 Bartlett pear, peeled, cored, and thinly sliced

MAKES 4 SERVINGS

Chill the salt bowls in the refrigerator for at least 2 hours. If the salt bowls are new, be sure to rub them thoroughly with a moist kitchen towel before using to bring out their luminous color.

Mix the red wine vinegar, olive oil, garlic, and pepper with a small whisk in a small bowl. Set aside.

Combine the radicchio, Belgian endives, escarole, chicory, basil, parsley, and chives in a large bowl. If not serving immediately, keep refrigerated until ready to serve.

To serve, put a portion of salad in each of the chilled salt bowls. Drizzle each salad with 2 teaspoons of the dressing and toss with your hands to glaze the greens with dressing. Scatter a tablespoon each of pomegranate seeds and blue cheese over each salad. Set a few pear slices on one side of each salad and drizzle with the remaining vinaigrette. Serve immediately.

Salt-Sloughed Butter (with Radishes, Brioche, and Fresh Peas)

Some people like it old school. If you made it past the word *sloughed* in this recipe title, you are one of them. The exquisite rural French snack of radishes and salted butter usually calls for unsalted butter topped with a pinch of excellent sea salt such as fleur de sel. But spread across the cool face of a salt block, soft butter gets just a lick of salt, and the radishes resting on the salt block pick up a bit of salt all for themselves. Combined, the flavor is a new classic.

1 (4 by 8 by 2-inch or 6 by 6 by 1½-inch) salt block

1 cup shelled English spring peas

1 bunch spring radishes, like French Breakfast or Icicle

4 ounces (1 stick) unsalted European-style butter, softened

6 brioche rolls, or 6 slices brioche-style bread, such as challah

MAKES 6 SERVINGS

Chill the salt block in the freezer for 5 to 10 minutes. Preheat the oven on low heat.

Meanwhile, bring 4 cups water to a boil in a small saucepan. Add the peas and boil until bright green, about 3 minutes. Drain the peas and run under cold water to stop the cooking. Set aside.

Trim the radishes of their greens and spindly roots; cut into thin slices. Set aside.

Remove the block from the freezer. Put the butter on the salt block and, using a stiff rubber or wooden spatula, smash the butter across the face of the salt block, smearing it into an even layer that almost covers the surface. Immediately scrape it into a mound in one corner of the block. Using the flat side of the spatula, mold the butter into a pyramid or a miniature Taj Mahal. Alternately, scrape up the salt with a teaspoon to make shavings of crested butter.

Fan rows of radish slices radiating out from the butter monument across the salt block. Perch the peas between the radish slices. Warm the brioche lightly in the oven.

Smear torn pieces of warm brioche into the freshly salted butter, add a pea or three, and roof it with a few radish shingles. Cleave it between your teeth for bright bursts of springtime.

Salt Block Ceviche of Scallops, Snapper, and Shrimp

Ceviche is a masterpiece of culinary engineering that even the most inventive molecular gastronomic whiz could never hope to rival. Acid and salt do the double duty of cooking the fish while also flavoring it with sour-sweet succulence, and a few peppers and herbs finish things off with some fireworks. The ingredients are firing on all cylinders. But where traditional ceviche relies on the citrus acid to do the curing, salt block ceviche summons salt. The fish takes on a heartier texture and richer flavor, and the bright, fresh flavors of the dressing bring everything miraculously to life.

1 (9-inch) square or round salt block

1 (8-ounce) fillet red snapper

4 dry-packed diver scallops

6 jumbo (U15 count) shrimp, peeled and deveined

Finely grated zest and juice of 1 lemon

Finely grated zest and juice of 2 limes

1 serrano or jalapeño chile pepper, stemmed, seeded, and finely diced

1 small plum tomato, stemmed, seeded, and finely diced

1 tablespoon finely chopped fresh cilantro leaves

A few coarse grinds of black pepper

MAKES 6 SERVINGS

Place the salt block on a rimmed baking sheet and put the snapper skin side down on the salt block. Refrigerate for 1 hour; the edges of the fish should start turning opaque.

While the fish is curing, remove the hard muscles from the sides of the scallops, and slice each scallop into 3 disks. Slice each shrimp lengthwise into thirds. After the snapper has finished curing, arrange the scallops and shrimp slices in a single layer around the fish. Pack the slices tightly against one another; there should be no salt block showing between the seafood pieces. Drizzle everything with the lemon and lime juices, being careful to keep the juices on the seafood, not on the salt block. Refrigerate for 1 hour longer; everything will turn opaque, but the texture of everything will still be fairly soft.

When the seafood is done curing, transfer the snapper to a cutting board and cut into thin slices against the grain; return to the salt block. Scatter everything with the lemon and lime zests, diced chile and tomato, chopped cilantro leaves, and several grinds of black pepper to taste. Serve immediately.

Smoked Salmon and Fresh Salmon Carpaccio Meet on a Salt Block Platter

The youth find nothing more insupportable than the old: their wizened ways, their old-fashioned dancing, their Nick Cave, their emphasis on flossing. But then there's the indulgent way the old don't bother to call the young on all their baloney. Smoked salmon has seen a thing or two on its long road to the table. It could teach fresh salmon carpaccio something about flavor, smoke-craft, love, fish oils, the ways of the word. Or it could invite the fresh salmon to a salt block and just watch what happens.

1 (8 by 12 by 2-inch, 10 by 10 by 2-inch) salt block platter

1 shallot, minced

1 garlic clove, minced

1 tablespoon finely grated fresh ginger

¼ teaspoon crushed red pepper flakes

¼ teaspoon ground coriander

¼ teaspoon freshly ground black pepper

1 tablespoon fresh lemon juice

1 tablespoon extra-virgin olive oil, plus more for pounding

6 ounces wild salmon fillet, cut into 6 (½-inch-thick) slices

3 ounces smoked wild salmon fillet, cut into 6 (⅛-inch-thick) slices

2 tablespoons chopped fresh flat-leaf parsley

1 lemon, thinly sliced, for garnish

MAKES 6 SERVINGS

Chill the salt block platter in the refrigerator for at least 2 hours.

Mix the shallot, garlic, ginger, red pepper flakes, coriander, black pepper, lemon juice, and the 1 tablespoon olive oil in a small bowl. Set aside.

Just before serving, pound out the fish: Drizzle a slice with a few drops of olive oil and rub over the fish. Place the oiled slice between two sheets of plastic wrap and gently pound into a wide, paper-thin sheet. I like to use a rubber mallet for pounding fish rather than a metal meat pounder, because it is less likely to tear the delicate muscle fibers. To get the thinnest possible slices, start pounding in the center, working your way out toward the edges. Use the old smack-and-slide motion, deflecting the hammer toward the edge of the slice as you bring it down. This will encourage the slice to spread in the direction of your movement rather than be crushed under a direct blow. Repeat with the remaining slices.

To serve, remove the top sheet of plastic from each slice and place in a shingle pattern over the surface of the cold salt block, alternating fresh and smoked fish, starting with a slice of fresh salmon and ending with a smoked slice. To place each slice, use the bottom piece of plastic as a support and flip the fish slice over onto the block; then peel off the plastic. Dress each slice with a little bit of the reserved sauce after you place it on the block. After all of the slices are arranged, top with the remaining sauce and the parsley. Garnish with the lemon slices.

A Capella Salt Block Antipasto

The meats, cheeses, and fruits of antipasti are best left unadorned to sing simply their songs of flavor and texture. But even these shining stars can benefit from a little acoustic help, and what better stage than a thick slab of antediluvian salt? Salt blocks dissolve under moist foods like mozzarella or Parmesan ice cream, lending an animating lick of liquid salt. Cured meats and hard cheeses, which have precious little available moisture, hardly change at all on a salt block. The block is just a candescent bulk of saltiness against which your thoughts can reverberate in harmony with your appetite.

1 (8 by 8 by 2-inch to 10 by 10 by 2-inch or 9-inch round) salt block

1 cup balsamic vinegar

4 ounces dry-cured salami, thinly sliced

4 fresh figs, halved lengthwise

4 small scoops Parmesan Ice Cream (page 174) or 4 medium-size mozzarella balls

2 tablespoons cold-pressed walnut oil

Slices of crusty bread, for serving

MAKES 4 SERVINGS

Chill the salt block in the freezer for at least 2 hours.

While the block is freezing, boil the balsamic vinegar in a small skillet over medium heat until it is reduced to one-third of its volume and is just thick enough to coat a spoon. Set aside.

Shingle the salami on one end of the salt block. Slice the fig halves lengthwise, leaving the slices attached at the stem end. Put on the other end of the salt block, cut side down, slices slightly splayed. Make a small pyramid of ice cream scoops in the center of the brick.

Drizzle the ice cream (or everything) with the cooled balsamic syrup and the oil. Serve immediately with plenty of crusty bread.

Salt Bowl Mayo and Variations: Aioli, Real Russian Dressing, and Sauce Fines Herbes

The mental image of mayonnaise in our collective consciousness is probably beyond saving. We have a hard time getting past the idea of it as jarred white stuff of indeterminate origin used in the interstices of a dish, something to glue odd bits of food together in a salad or sandwich. But handmade mayo has its own raison d'être, a purpose both huge and immutable: It gives us a dip so delicious that it gets us to eat our raw vegetables without complaint. Making it in a salt bowl magically coaxes just the right amount of salt into the mayo to make it come alive, and it makes a beautiful presentation to boot. Make any one of these mayonnaises separately, or make all four and serve side by side with anything from fresh vegetables to a shellfish platter; or try my favorite, dolloped over hard-boiled eggs.

1 (2- to 3-cup) salt bowl

2 egg yolks (large or extra-large)

2 teaspoons Dijon mustard

2 tablespoons fresh lemon juice

¾ cup mild vegetable oil, such as safflower, peanut, or sunflower

¼ cup olive oil

1 tablespoon boiling water

Freshly ground white or black pepper

MAKES 1⅓ CUPS; ⅓ CUP
(4 SERVINGS) OF EACH VARIETY

Place the egg yolks and mustard in the salt block bowl, and beat with a whisk until well combined. Mix in the lemon juice, and add the oils in a slow, steady stream, mixing constantly until thick and creamy. Stir in the boiling water and season with pepper to taste.

AIOLI

1 small garlic clove, minced

½ cup Salt Bowl Mayo

Stir the garlic into the prepared mayonnaise. Serve immediately (with crudités, cold boiled potatoes, or grilled seafood).

REAL RUSSIAN DRESSING

2 teaspoons tomato paste

1 tablespoon sour cream

½ cup Salt Bowl Mayo

1 tablespoon salmon caviar

Stir the tomato paste and sour cream into the prepared mayonnaise. Fold in the caviar; serve immediately (on hard-boiled eggs, crudités, or toasted black bread).

SAUCE FINES HERBES

1 teaspoon finely chopped fresh flat-leaf parsley

1 teaspoon finely chopped fresh tarragon

1 teaspoon finely chopped fresh chives

1 teaspoon finely chopped fresh chervil

½ cup Salt Bowl Mayo

Stir the parsley, tarragon, chives, and chervil into the prepared mayonnaise. Serve immediately (with crudités or poached and chilled vegetables).

CHAPTER 2

CURING ON (AND BETWEEN) SALT BLOCKS

Do you feel the need for speed? It's so much a part of our lives that we no longer see speed for what it is: probably the single best invention of the modern age. Where once upon a time mud sucked our boots as we plodded down rutted roads for weeks every day on the way to school, now autumn leaves trail in the wake of our giddy velocity as we blaze down sidewalks on Rollerblades. Speed is nice: It feels nice, it looks nice, and with salt blocks, it tastes nice. Salt-preserved lemons that take a month to do in the traditional technique are done in a day! And if you have a tough time planning meals weeks and months out, this same speed allows you to cook more of the fun foods you want to cook, when you want to enjoy them.

Curing with salt blocks is definitely an example of a situation where two things add up to more than the sum of their parts; using two blocks to cure food is a case in point. The surface area is doubled, so you have salt working to cure the food item from both sides. In addition, the weight of the block on the food has a major role in affecting the cure. As the salt goes to work in the food, breaking down cells and releasing the moisture, the weight of the block presses the newly available moisture out of the food.

Not only does this accelerate the cure but it also improves the texture. This is because blocks are very different from salt granules. Where loose salt crystals draw out and sponge up moisture, salt blocks offer a solid two-dimensional face, so they draw moisture only very subtly. The effect on food can be dazzling.

Curing watermelon into a ham that you can then wrap around melon (see page 75) can only be achieved with salt blocks, and the flavor and texture of this dish alone validates the entire concept of curing with salt blocks.

Curing foods with salt blocks also brings home what so often we farm out. All the lovely condiments and prepared foods we pull from jars and deli wrappers once came from home kitchens. We preserved tart summer fruits and later in the year brought the antioxidant- and vitamin-rich nutrients of summer to winter meals. Salt-cured meats provided an economical and convenient way to add hearty complexity to meals year-round. Salt blocks bring this rustic tradition into the fast-paced contemporary home, letting us salt-cure a fresh lemon (see page 82) in the morning and use it on roast leg of lamb in the evening. The exquisite and very fancy hors d'oeuvres you might buy at an upscale market can instead be the gravlax (see page 66) you just made yourself.

Then there's the convenience. Curing can be laborious, requiring special vessels, packing salt, draining foods, unpacking salt, rinsing foods, and so on. Salt block curing is often incredibly easy. Slap cucumber onto the block with some aromatics, and before you know it you have a remarkable cucumber salad (see page 69). Many of the foods that are cured with salt blocks take on enough salt to make them great elements in other dishes, where they contribute seasoning in addition to the flavor of the ingredient. Try stirring spiced beef leather (see page 80) into scrambled eggs or pasta sauce. Top steamed rice with a little vegetable pickle (see page 72).

Buying two salt blocks for a curing recipe might seem like an expensive proposition, but you can do dozens of cures, and prepare an endless variety of recipes, using the same two salt blocks. In other words, they represent a rather abstract cost, which can only be calculated as a factor of the lifespan of the block, sort of like factoring the cost of a waffle iron to the cost of your waffle. Except you can do way more than waffles on a salt block.

Also, you need not pay a lot for salt blocks used for curing. At my store we sell a tableware-graded line of salt blocks that are specially selected for serving and curing, offered at roughly half the cost of salt blocks graded for cooking. Some other retailers have followed suit. There is no need to pay top dollar for a salt block graded for cooking when it is never going to be subjected to intense heat. On the flip side, you can go ahead and buy the more expensive, cookware-graded blocks and use them for curing several times, and then later decide to start cooking on them without harming the blocks—or voiding the warranty. It doesn't work the other way around, though. Once you cook on a salt block, it is best to stick to cooking on it, as the micro-fissures that form under heat will lead the block to take on too much moisture during a cure, over-curing your food and more rapidly breaking down your salt block.

Sometimes salt blocks are for making something taste delicious. Sometimes they're for creating beauty. Sometimes they are for fun. Sometimes they are all of those things. When it comes to the serious business of curing, they are quite simply a technically superior way to get the job done. From artichoke heart to zebra heart, salt blocks offer fast, easy, and dazzlingly effective ways to cure.

THE CHEMISTRY OF CURING

The process of curing food encompasses a vast field of expertise because there are so many foods that can be preserved, and just about every one of these foods has many different ways to preserve it. Salt, pH, redox potential, high- and low-temperature processing, and additives can all be enlisted in the battle against decay—alone or, more often, in combination. Each of these requires very precise methods and a high degree of control over the process, so there are technical limits to the ways you can cure with the willing but unwieldy salt block.

Salt block curing fits into two basic categories: quick cures, where the salt draws out a modest amount of moisture and increases the salinity of the food just enough to improve its texture and taste while extending the life of the food, often with the aid of refrigeration; and full cures, where salt is brought into greater contact with the food to draw out more moisture and raise salinity to create cures that can last for long periods of time without refrigeration. With a quick cure like gravlax, no more than 10 percent of the food's moisture will be lost. With a slow cure such as beef jerky, upward of 30 percent of the food's moisture may be lost.

There are limits to what you can cure with salt blocks, or at least major technical constraints, simply because salt alone is not always the best way to go about a cure. A little curing science will explain. Salt all by itself works as a preservative because it reduces the amount of water available for microbial growth and chemical reactions. It is believed that sodium and chloride ions associate closely with water molecules, keeping them occupied and reducing the amount of activity that can occur in the water. This prohibits certain chemical reactions that cause decay and it puts microbes into osmotic shock, inhibiting their growth or killing them outright. That is a salt cure.

But many cures benefit from other preservation agents in addition to salt. Acidity (pH), redox potential, and high- or low-temperature processing and storage are also important tools in preservation. Dried sausages, for example, use fermentation to increase acidity (lower pH) enough to inhibit the growth of dangerous bacteria like *Clostridium botulinum* (a kind of food poisoning). In fermented sausages, salt is mixed evenly throughout the meat to preserve everything just long enough to allow the fermentation process to take hold. Salt and acidity work as a team. Without the aid of these desirable, fermenting bacteria, it would take three to four times more salt than is palatable to cure a sausage! Achieving the right mix of salt, air, and fermenting bacterial growth using a salt block would be a real doozy.

Quick Salt Cod

Quickness is relative. A quick cup of coffee means a matter of minutes, a quick dinner happens in less than half an hour, but a quick cure can take weeks. Salt cod (baccala) typically cures in salt for months, so reducing the process to a few days is nothing less than revolutionary. Salt cod is a mainstay of the Mediterranean, appearing in every cuisine from Portuguese to Tunisian. This quick-cure method is like finding a magical trap door that opens into a whole region of sun-drenched cuisines. You will need to soak it in three or four changes of cold water for about 12 hours total to rid it of salt before cooking with it. Use it in any salt cod recipe. It is delicious simmered with tomatoes and potatoes.

2 (8 to 10-inch) square or (9-inch) round salt blocks

2 pounds cod fillet, cut into 8 (4-ounce) slices no thicker than ½ inch

MAKES 8 SERVINGS

Place a salt block on a baking sheet to catch any drips. Wash the cod in cold water and pat dry. Put the fish slices in a single layer on the block. Top with the other block. Cover with plastic wrap and refrigerate for 24 hours.

Remove the cod from between the blocks. Blot it dry with paper towels. Wrap each piece of dried cod in a sheet of paper towel and put in a plastic bag; do not seal the bag. Refrigerate for at least 72 hours or up to 2 weeks, changing the paper towels every 24 hours. The longer the fish cures, the less perishable it will be. After 2 weeks it should be bone-dry, and at that point it may be stored in the refrigerator in a zipper lock bag for up to 6 months. Once it is completely dry the fish no longer needs to be wrapped in paper towels.

Soak in several changes of cold water to rehydrate and desalinate before cooking.

Salt Block Cured Gravlax

Life isn't all Champagne and caviar, as they say. And who would want it to be? Pizza and rosé after a day playing Frisbee; guacamole, chips, and beer at home watching the Super Bowl; bouillabaisse and a solid Grenache after a long hike up and down a misty coastal mountain. Homemade gravlax and a glass of sparkling wine is a decadent celebration anytime. And making it on a salt block is so easy, so delicious, and so rewarding that you may start believing that life really is all Champagne and caviar after all.

2 (8 by 12 by 2-inch or 9 by 9 by 2-inch) salt block platters

1 bunch dill sprigs

2 teaspoons coarsely ground black pepper

1 teaspoon cracked fennel seeds

½ teaspoon dried thyme

¼ cup sugar

1 pound skin-on salmon fillet, pin-bones removed

Whole-grain crackers, for serving

Crème fraîche, for garnish

Chopped fresh dill, for garnish

MAKES 6 SERVINGS

Lay half the dill sprigs over one of the salt block platters.

Combine the pepper, fennel seeds, thyme, and sugar in a small bowl. Pat the seasoning mixture onto the fleshy parts of the salmon until thoroughly covered. Place the coated salmon on the dill-covered salt block and cover with the remaining half of the dill sprigs. Place the other salt block platter on top. You are now looking at a slab of salmon sandwiched between two lambent salt blocks. Wrap the whole thing in plastic wrap. Refrigerate until the fish feels resilient but not quite firm to the touch. Visually, it should appear dry on the surface but moist and oily inside. A thin fillet of wild salmon will take 1 day to cure, while a thick fillet of farmed salmon will take up to 3 days.

When the gravlax is ready, unwrap the setup, remove the fish from between the salt blocks. Rinse lightly to remove the seasoning, and pat dry. Put the salmon on a cutting board, skin side down, and starting at the wider end slice thinly on a slant.

Serve with crackers (or blinis or toast points, over soft-scrambled eggs, or solo). A dollop of crème fraîche and a garnish of dill are always welcome.

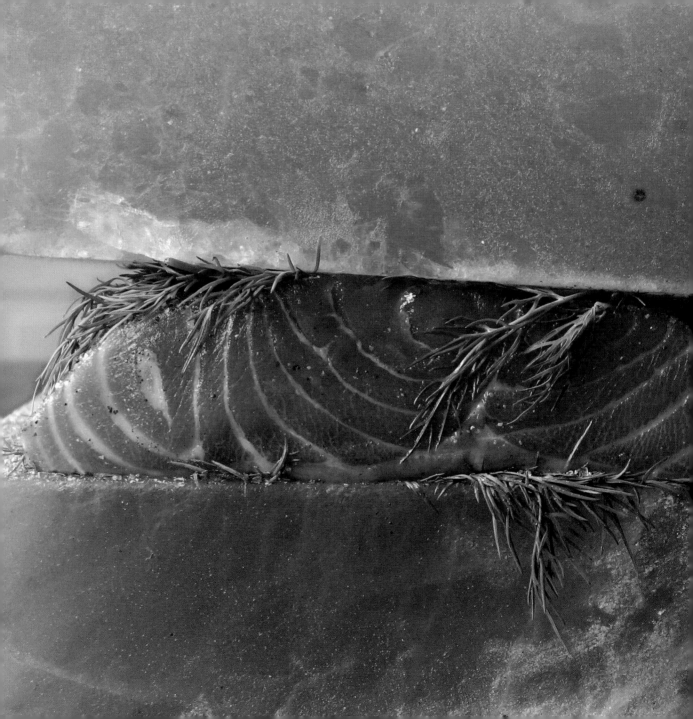

Salt Block Cucumber Salad

Many eaters of the cucumber have a love-hate relationship with it. Peeling them removes most of their flavor, color, and texture, but not peeling can leave a touch too much bitterness, toughness, and waxiness. They have a nice crunch, but they can be watery and unsatisfying. Salt blocks offer a solution to this dilemma and guarantee a supremely satisfying cucumber-eating experience. Seek out cucumbers with tender, mild, unwaxed peels such as Kirby or English varieties, then give them a quick cure on the old salt block. This firms the cucumber's texture, concentrates its delicate flavor, and mellows the intensity of the peel. Once you have given your cucumbers the right kind of attention, anything you decide to do with them will be dilemma-free deliciousness. Consider doubling this recipe so there will be more for tomorrow.

1 (8 by 12 by 2-inch or 10 by 10 by 2-inch) salt block

4 small (unwaxed Kirby (or 2 medium English cucumbers), cut in ¼-inch-thick slices

2 tablespoons extra-virgin olive oil

1 small garlic clove, minced

¼ small red onion, finely chopped

¼ teaspoon freshly ground black pepper

1 tablespoon rice wine vinegar or white wine vinegar

2 tablespoons chopped fresh dill

MAKES 4 SERVINGS

Arrange the cucumber slices in a single layer on the salt block, as though setting up a checkers board (you will have to do this in batches). Let sit for 2 minutes. Flip the slices and let cure for another 1 minute. Remove the cucumber slices from the block and put in a clean, lint-free kitchen towel. Wrap the towel around the cucumber slices and wring purposefully but gently to remove any excess moisture. Put the cucumbers in a serving bowl. Wipe off the block and repeat the process with the remaining cucumber slices.

Add the olive oil, garlic, onion, black pepper, vinegar, and dill to the bowl. Toss to coat the cucumber slices evenly. Serve immediately, or refrigerate for up to 2 days.

Salt-Cured Candied Strawberries

Let your mind wander through a bursting bright berry patch of flavors. How do you improve on the sunny perfection of a ripe strawberry? The answer lies in a wonderfully brutal combination of sweetness, saltiness, and pressure. Rubbed with cane sugar and sandwiched by salt blocks, flavors concentrate and aromas break free. Under the block's unyielding pressure, salt merges into sweet, wringing boldness from delicacy. This new sweetly acidic-salty combination does us all the favor of increasing a strawberry's otherwise somewhat limited versatility. Try it in a balsamic duck spring roll, with chocolate mousse, atop a cracker with goat cheese, or garnishing a post-tequila shot of sangrita. Ridding a berry of most of its water focuses its flavor like a ruby captures lamplight, exposing a more palpable essence that was hiding in plain sight.

2 (4 by 8 by 2-inch or 8 by 8 by 2-inch) salt blocks

8 large perfect strawberries with greens attached

4 cups sugar

MAKES 4 SERVINGS

Place one of the salt blocks on a rimmed baking sheet to catch any drips from the strawberries.

Space the strawberries evenly in a single layer on the block. Carefully place the other salt block squarely on top so that it balances evenly on all of the strawberries. Set aside until the berries are lightly compressed, 2 to 3 hours, depending on ripeness. As the strawberries cure, they will lose about 50 percent of their water, concentrating their flavor.

Pat the strawberries dry with paper towels and toss very gently on a plate with the sugar. Use as a garnish with ice cream, cake, or cookies; or serve with an excellent chocolate bar. You may store the berries, covered, in the refrigerator for up to 12 hours. If the berries become damp, dry them with paper towels and dust them again with sugar.

Quick-Cured Vegetable Pickles

Toward the end of summer one of two things can happen. Either you are scarfing down steamed summer squash like there's no tomorrow—because indeed tomorrow there will be no more—or you are feeling like it's high time for something a little different. Either way, a salt block will convert those fresh vegetables into a beautiful pickle that eases you into an autumnal frame of mind. Added vinegar mimics the acidity that would normally arise from fermentation. Olive oil inhibits the salt's desire to take over. This teamwork pays off with pickled vegetables softened and seasoned but still crisp and fresh. The miracle of the salt block is that the pickle takes hours rather than days. You'll like them plain, and you'll love them with everything from steamed rice to chicken curry to steak tartare (page 41) to a hamburger.

1 (8- to 10-inch) square or (9-inch) round salt block

3 tablespoons apple cider vinegar

1 tablespoon light brown sugar

1 garlic clove, minced

1 teaspoon minced fresh ginger

10 coriander seeds, toasted (see Note) and crushed

2 Asian eggplant or small Mediterranean eggplant, cut into ¼-inch-thick rounds

or

3 zucchini or yellow squash, cut into ¼-inch-thick diagonal slices

or

2 medium unwaxed English cucumbers, cut into ¼-inch-thick diagonal slices

MAKES 4 SERVINGS

Mix the vinegar, brown sugar, garlic, ginger, and coriander in a large bowl.

Toss the vegetable (or vegetables) of your choice in the vinegar mixture. Arrange on the salt block in a single layer. If using eggplant, cure for 1 hour, turning the eggplant slices halfway through. If using squash or cucumber, cure for 40 minutes, turning the slices halfway through. When the vegetables are cured, they will be flexible but still firm. Remove from the block, and pat dry with paper towels. If you like, cut the pickle slices into smaller pieces. Serve immediately, or store covered in the refrigerator for up to 1 week.

NOTE: To toast coriander (or any whole spice), heat a heavy skillet, preferably cast iron, over high heat for 5 minutes. Remove from the heat, add the spice to the dry skillet, and toss until the spice is aromatic and barely colored, usually about 30 seconds. Remove from the skillet and use as desired.

Watermelon Ham and Melon

If you haven't tried it, sprinkle a pinch of fleur de sel on a wedge of watermelon right now. It's incredible. Down South this is the traditional way to eat watermelon. Salting cantaloupe or honeydew doesn't evoke the same spine-tingling response. The scientific explanation for this is because watermelon is naturally low in sodium. One cup of cantaloupe has 26 grams of sodium. One cup of honeydew has 31 grams. By comparison, 1 cup of watermelon has just 2 grams. The naturally occurring salt in cantaloupe and honeydew tames their sugars and at the same time heightens their flavors. That's why watermelon tastes sweeter than cantaloupe or honeydew even though it is lower in sugar. A little salt on that watermelon tames the sugars and sends the flavor through the roof. Curing thin strips of watermelon between two salt blocks boosts it clear out of the produce kingdom and lands it somewhere else entirely, turning your fruit into the most delectable "prosciutto." Maybe science can explain everything, but don't let anyone tell you there's no such thing as magic.

2 (4 by 8 by 2-inch or 8 by 8 by 2-inch) salt blocks

8 (¼-inch-thick) slices watermelon quarters, rinds removed

½ teaspoon coarsely ground dried green peppercorns

¼ teaspoon freshly ground black pepper

8 thin wedges honeydew melon or cantaloupe, rinds removed, chilled

MAKES 4 SERVINGS

Place one of the salt blocks on a wire rack set on a rimmed baking sheet that will catch the water that is going to flow from the watermelon.

Put the watermelon slices in stacks of two evenly spaced on the salt block. Carefully place the other block squarely on top so that it balances evenly on the watermelon slices. Set aside until the watermelon slices are compressed by half, about 2 hours. As the watermelon slices cure, they will lose about 50 percent of their water, concentrating their flavor.

Remove the watermelon from between the salt blocks. It will feel fleshy, like raw tuna. Blot the slices on paper towels and sprinkle each slice on both sides with the green peppercorns and black pepper. If not serving immediately, refrigerate until ready to serve.

To serve, wrap each honeydew wedge with a piece of watermelon "prosciutto" and serve. If you prefer, you may cut the honeydew into chunks and the watermelon into strips; drape a strip over each chunk and serve sushi-style.

Preserved Savage Mushrooms

Mushrooms grow fast, but they cure even faster. Unlike plants and animals, which grow by cell division, mushrooms grow by cell enlargement. All they need is a little stored energy and a lot of water and they're good to go from button-size to baseball-size in a matter of days. This means mushrooms are anywhere from 65 percent to 95 percent water, depending on the variety. They're saturated sponges, so shouldering them with the weight of a block forces out the water. Lickety-split, mushrooms become meaty, chewy, condensed things. This happens with such alacrity it's incredible—a more radical and rapid metamorphosis than their vigorous growth. Toss them in oil, herbs, and garlic to keep the salt in check and to give the meaty mushrooms some love after so much miraculous transformation. Toss with fresh pasta, pile on bruschetta, or fold into a tangy civet of rabbit.

2 (8- to 10-inch) square or (9-inch) round salt blocks

6 ounces wild mushrooms, such as oyster, shiitake, morel, cèpe, or chanterelle

Leaves from 2 large fresh rosemary sprigs

2 garlic cloves, minced

¼ cup extra-virgin olive oil

Juice of 1 lime

MAKES 4 SERVINGS

Place one of the salt blocks on a rimmed baking sheet to catch any drips from the mushrooms.

If the mushrooms are large or thick, cut into ¼-inch-thick slices. If they are thin, like oyster mushrooms or small chanterelles, leave them whole. Toss the mushrooms, rosemary, garlic, and olive oil together in a bowl until the mushrooms are evenly coated.

Spread the mushrooms on the block in an even layer. Top with the other salt block and let cure for about 10 minutes.

Transfer the mushrooms from the blocks to a bowl and stir in the lime juice. Store covered in the refrigerator for up to 3 days.

Sun-Dried Salt Block Tomatoes

A tomato plucked right out of the hot sunshine from the raised bed in your backyard is so unlike a store-bought hothouse tomato that it's a wonder we even call them by the same name. Slicing garden tomatoes is like butchering—the flavor they release is a disconcerting combination of warm flesh and meaty vegetable. With two salt blocks and some sunshine you can invoke the same backyard experience—no green thumb required. Placing salt blocks in direct sunlight will warm them to in excess of 100°F. Combining this heat with the weight and salinity of the blocks releases moisture from the tomatoes, concentrating their essence to produce massive flavor from any tomato, whether it's the garden variety or otherwise. The somewhat assertive level of salt makes them perfect whole or minced in salads, pastas, soups, burritos, omelets, or over full-flavored meats such as beef, lamb, and game. Warm, sunny weather is required for this recipe.

2 (8- to 10-inch) square or (9-inch) round salt blocks

6 plum tomatoes, halved lengthwise

1 tablespoon extra-virgin olive oil

MAKES 12 PIECES, ABOUT 1½ CUPS

Place one of the salt blocks on a rimmed baking sheet to catch the moisture that will weep from the tomatoes as they dry.

Coat the cut sides of the tomatoes with the olive oil and put the tomatoes, cut side down, on the block. Top with the other block and wrap cheesecloth around the perimeter of the blocks to protect the open area between the blocks from insects. Put the whole shebang outside on a table in the warm sunshine until the tomatoes have lost about half their moisture, are wrinkled and flattened, and have become about ½ inch thick. The blocks should get hot to the touch, and depending on the temperature, the tomatoes should be ready in 2 to 4 hours.

Remove the tomatoes from the blocks, pat dry, and store in the refrigerator for up to 1 month. Use as you would sun-dried tomatoes.

Salt-Tanned Spiced Beef Leather

Chipped beef on toast, basically very thin slices of salted beef stirred into a roux, is a vanishing mainstay of American cuisine—pushed aside by that retro classic of classics, biscuits and sausage gravy. I think this is a reflection on the poor quality of the chipped beef rather than on any inherent superiority of pork sausage. Pounding the beef out results in super-quick dehydration, but by keeping the cure quick, only a moderate amount of moisture is lost. The cure is achieved through adding salt rather than by removing water. The resulting jerky can be stored in the refrigerator for several weeks. It is chewy, with a very satisfying texture and bright red color. The flavor is intentionally highly seasoned, both in spice and salt. This makes for more a condiment than a snack food. The beef leather is good with pasta, mashed potatoes, or rice, or in salads, pasta sauces, or potato salads. Or serve it on toast with gravy and see how it stacks up to chipped beef or B&G.

2 (8 by 12 by 2-inch) salt block platters or 6 (4 by 8 by 2-inch) salt blocks

1 teaspoon smoked paprika

¼ teaspoon ground smoked black pepper

Pinch of ground chipotle chile pepper

2 teaspoons light brown sugar

8 ounces flank steak

MAKES 4 SERVINGS

Mix the smoked paprika, smoked black pepper, chipotle chile, and sugar in a small bowl.

Cut the flank steak in half with the grain. Slice each half at a 45-degree angle as thinly as you can against the grain. Sprinkle the slices on both sides with the spice mixture.

Working with two or three slices at a time, put the slices on a cutting board and cover with a sheet of plastic wrap. Pound them with a smooth meat mallet or a rubber hammer into paper-thin sheets. Remove the plastic wrap and arrange on one of the salt block platters in a single layer, packed together as tightly as possible without overlapping slices. Repeat with all of the meat slices.

Put the other salt block platter on top. Wrap the whole salt block sandwich in aluminum foil or plastic wrap and refrigerate until the beef slices are firm and chewy, about 24 hours.

Remove the meat from the block, pat dry, and store covered in the refrigerator for up to 2 weeks. Use as you would any dried beef—hashed with potatoes, tossed with pasta and sauce, and so on.

Salt Block Preserved Lemon Slices

Few things are more simultaneously exasperating and amusing than a child opening up an expensive holiday gift and then categorically rejecting the toy in favor of the box the toy came in. We have an innate knack for sussing out the authentically good stuff. The toy: a poorly constructed product created by focus groups. The box: an engineering marvel tasked with holding, protecting, and transporting it. The same can be said of lemons. Their skin is a marvel that we too often mistake for mere packaging. The peels are burgeoning with Middle Eastern notes of citrus oil and bitter tannin. Curing them with salt releases the juice from the pulp and turns the bitter peel into the mild, tender, scrumptious center of attention. Curing with salt blocks achieves in two days what takes traditional salt curing a month. Slice these up to top grilled foods, stews, sauces, couscous, and many Middle Eastern dishes.

2 (8- to 10-inch) square or (9-inch) round salt blocks

2 large lemons, cut into ⅛- to ¼-inch-thick rounds

Juice of 1 lemon

MAKES 2 CUPS

Place one of the salt blocks on a wire rack set on a rimmed baking sheet to catch the juices extracted from the lemons.

Arrange the lemon slices evenly spaced in a single layer on the salt block. Carefully place the other block on top. Let cure until the rinds on the lemon slices are chewy, about 48 hours. As the lemon slices cure, they will lose about 50 percent of their water, concentrating their flavor.

Remove the lemon slices from between the salt blocks. They will feel fleshy. Put the slices in a container and cover with a combination of 50 percent lemon juice and water. Store in a closed container in the refrigerator for up to 1 month. Use in any recipe that calls for preserved lemon.

CHAPTER 3

WARMING ON SALT BLOCKS AND IN SALT BOWLS

Gorgonzola–Olive Oil Queso with Dipping Figs

Molten Brie with Pistachio Crumbs and Warm Salted Dates

Warm Black Bean Dip

Chèvre Brûlée and Arugula Wilted on Warm Salt with Pears

Salt-Melted Chocolate Fondue with Crisp Bacon

Bagna Cauda Warmed in a Salt Bowl, Served with Artichokes

Salt Block Smashed Potatoes

Salt Block Raclette with Fire-Roasted New Potatoes and Shallots

We've been eating salt for a long time—in fact, deciding just how we've been eating it depends on how you define we. Ever since we became modern human beings some 200,000 years ago, our physiological need for salt has shaped where we have lived and what we have eaten. We followed animals to salt deposits, ate the animals, and then ate the salt. Eventually, as we became more sophisticated, we ate the animals and the salt at the same time, and the first cuisine was born! For hundreds of millennia before the dog was first domesticated, salt has been our steadfast best friend—as a nutrient, a seasoning, and a preservative. Now it's time to look to salt for something new.

Audacious statement of dazzling insight: Food is often tastier served warm. And yes, food is even better warmed up and salted. Food that is warmed and salted on salt is the bomb. Different foods seem to take just what they need. Try warming chèvre brûlée and arugula (see page 94) on the block together so the salt and the warmth both can work their wizardry on each type of food, each in their own way. So imagine our good luck to find that salt is not only the king of seasoning, but also an absolutely top-notch hot plate to boot.

It turns out that salt's molecular properties in the world of taste are rivaled by its properties in the realm of energy. Salt has about twice the specific heat of steel, meaning you need to put about twice the amount of energy into a salt block to heat it up 1°F as you do your steel pan. Thus a salt block at 150°F is holding a lot more energy in it than a metal pan of the same weight,

so you can do things with it like heat it in the fire and then take it to the table to melt the divine Alpine cheese called raclette onto fire-roasted potatoes and cornichons (see page 102).

Salt also has very low thermal conductivity, so the energy that is in there is slow to come out. If you heat aluminum, the energy moves in quickly, and passes out quickly—that's why you can touch something right out of the oven if it's wrapped in aluminum foil. Energy passes through salt much more slowly, and conversely the heat is downright lackadaisical about coming back out.

Compounding their mule-like thermal stubbornness, salt blocks are five to ten times more massive than anything else you might have to serve food from in the kitchen. The upshot is that if you toss a salt block on the stove for 20 minutes, you will have something that will both warm and season bean dip (see page 91) or gorgonzola and olive oil queso (see page 87) at the same time, and it will do both of these things better than anything else on earth.

Apparently not done showing off, salt has one last property to flaunt, one that miraculously allows us to take full advantage of its warming and seasoning awesomeness. It can be shaped. A Himalayan salt rock can be turned on a lathe to make a rounded platter, or a dish, or even a bowl. This is the cooking utensil you have been waiting for: one simple pot for preparing, serving, and warming everything from bagna cauda (see page 98) to chocolate fondue (see page 96). Mankind's 200,000-year-long obsession with salt has evolved to a higher level.

Gorgonzola–Olive Oil Queso with Dipping Figs

Gulping whole raw milk straight from the cow pushes your senses to the precipice; it is bursting with such oleaginous, silken, bovine intensity that it is no wonder few of us even think to crave such indulgence. Or perhaps it's just that we're squeamish about wrapping our fingers around the disconcertingly soft, turgid udder of the cow to procure it. Warming Gorgonzola in a salt bowl re-creates something of the sinful extra-virgin flavor of raw milk. Gorgonzola cheese, which is made from unskimmed milk, faithfully preserves the cow's hugeness, and the warmth and salt from the salt bowl animates it with a vital moo. The plump figs, with their titillating softness, are the closest thing to an udder I can imagine.

1 (1- to 2-cup) salt bowl

2 tablespoons heavy cream or half-and-half

3 small oregano sprigs

4 ounces Gorgonzola dolce, cut and/or crumbled into small pieces

A few grinds of black pepper

1 tablespoon extra-virgin olive oil (the best you can afford)

12 fresh figs (black or green), quartered lengthwise

MAKES 6 SERVINGS

Place the salt bowl on a burner over very low heat to warm to about 200°F, about 30 minutes (see Read Before Heating!, page 25). If your burner doesn't go low enough, or you are using an electric burner, use a heat diffuser.

At the same time you set the bowl over the burner, remove the cream from the refrigerator to lose its chill.

When ready to serve, remove the bowl from the heat and put the cream and oregano in the salt bowl to warm for 1 minute. Add the cheese and stir until everything is melted and smooth. Stir in the pepper and olive oil. Serve the warm bowl of queso with the quartered figs for dipping.

Molten Brie with Pistachio Crumbs and Warm Salted Dates

When I was a teen, my father's favorite way to spend the day with us was to invite a few friends on a hike or a picnic where we would throw down a blanket, crack open iced bottles of Löwenbräu (it was always Löwenbräu) and open a nice, Velveeta-smooth disk of Brie cheese. He was a regular Cyrano de Bergerac with a cheese knife, and we always had to spar with him to get our share. Skip ahead 10 years. I was living in Paris when a friend at the Sorbonne invited me to dinner. There was something on the table, molten, alive, almost boozy to the nose, and it was creeping surreptitiously from the cutting board. "What in the heck is it?" I blurted out. "You don't like?" intoned my host. With my mouth crammed full of food, I didn't bother responding, but just scooped up some more. It was a farmhouse Brie, served at room temperature. A moment earlier I had considered myself a Brie connoisseur. A moment later I realized I had never even eaten the real stuff. Salt blocks, with their thermal mass and unassuming bulk, transform store-bought Brie into a crash course on the true flavor of good cheese.

1 (8-inch) square or (9-inch) round salt block, tempered (see page 30)

½ cup shelled unsalted pistachios, coarsely chopped

1 garlic clove, minced

1 egg yolk

2 tablespoons heavy cream

1 (6-ounce) wedge Brie, with rind

12 Medjool dates, pitted

Small pieces of toast, for serving (optional)

MAKES 4 SERVINGS

Place the tempered salt block on a baking sheet in the oven. Turn the oven to 200°F and let it preheat with the block inside (see Read Before Heating!, page 25).

Meanwhile, put the pistachios and garlic in the work bowl of a food processor equipped with a steel blade and process in pulses until the nuts are ground to the texture of cornmeal. Dump the nut mixture onto a sheet of aluminum foil or plastic wrap.

Mix the egg yolk and cream with a fork in a small bowl until smooth. Brush the cheese with the egg mixture and roll it in the pistachio crumbs until well coated on all sides.

Remove the warm block (still on its baking sheet) from the oven. Place the cheese and dates on the block and return to the oven. Warm until the cheese is just beginning to ooze and the dates feel warm to the touch, about 20 minutes.

Serve with toast, or just smear some cheese on a date and enjoy. The warm block will keep the cheese warm and oozy for about an hour.

Warm Black Bean Dip

It's practically axiomatic that the simplest, humblest dishes are often the best. But on the flip side, the simplest things can undercut even the best recipes. Bean dip is a case in point. Everybody loves bean dip, for its warm melty beany cheesiness, Tex-Mex seasoning, and guilt-free (this is flat-out health food) snackability. But within minutes of serving it, your dip is cold—and cold bean dip sucks. Enter the salt bowl. The bowl heats and seasons the dip, presents it with flair, and then keeps it warm—not for minutes, but for hours. There's no hurry to finish it. You can leave it on a table at a party, or when home alone, you can put on a game and take your sweet time with a whole bowl of perpetually warm dip waiting patiently for the next chip.

1 (2- to 3-cup) salt bowl

1 tablespoon olive oil

1 small yellow onion, finely chopped

1 medium tomato, cored and cut into medium dice

2 garlic cloves, minced

2 teaspoons ground toasted cumin

1 tablespoon apple cider vinegar

1 (15½-ounce) can black beans, rinsed and drained

1 canned chipotle chile in adobo, minced

2 tablespoons adobo sauce from the chipotles

Freshly ground black pepper

¼ to ⅓ cup hot water

¼ cup finely shredded Monterey Jack (1 ounce)

⅓ cup chopped fresh cilantro

Unsalted tortilla and/or corn chips, for dipping

MAKES 8 SERVINGS

Place the salt bowl on a burner over very low heat to warm to about 200°F, about 30 minutes (see Read Before Heating!, page 25). If your burner doesn't go low enough, or you are using an electric burner, use a heat diffuser.

Meanwhile, heat a medium skillet over medium-high heat. Add the olive oil and sauté the onion until transparent, about 2 minutes. Add the tomato, garlic, and cumin and sauté just until the cumin is aromatic and the tomato loses its raw look, about 3 minutes. Remove from the heat and stir in the vinegar; set aside.

When the salt bowl is warm, add the black beans and mash with a small fork or spoon into a coarse paste (there may still be a few whole beans visible). Stir in the chipotle chile and adobo sauce, black pepper, and ¼ cup hot water. Add the cheese and heat, stirring occasionally until the cheese melts, about 1 minute. Remove the bowl from the heat.

Stir in the sautéed vegetables. Add more of the hot water if needed to reach your desired consistency. Stir in the cilantro and serve the warm bowl of dip surrounded by chips for dipping.

Chèvre Brûlée and Arugula Wilted on Warm Salt with Pears

Cooking is an emotional experience, and because salting is a culinary fundamental, changing our notions of salting changes our emotional relationship to food at a primal level. Most of the time salt is either added during cooking, in which case its sensuality invades the food deeply, or it is scattered on the finished dish, creating a luster of flavor on the surface. Serving goat cheese on a warm salt block uses salt in yet a third way, raising the cheese's temperature and melting its fats to release all the unctuously feral flavors that previously lay cloaked in its chemistry. Because goat cheese has very little available moisture, the salt block barely seasons the cheese. Adding some moist fruit and salad to the block gives the salt an opportunity to shine in its seasoning role, providing just enough salinity to wrap everything up in a warm embrace.

1 (4 by 8 by 2-inch or 6 by 6 by 1½-inch) salt block, tempered (see page 30)

1 (4-ounce) log fresh goat cheese, halved, well chilled

1½ tablespoons light brown sugar

2 teaspoons extra-virgin olive oil

2 teaspoons red wine vinegar

½ garlic clove, smashed

2 ounces arugula

½ Bartlett pear, cored and thinly sliced

Small pieces of toast, for serving (optional)

MAKES 2 SERVINGS

Place the tempered salt block on a baking sheet in the oven. Turn the oven to 200°F and let it preheat with the block inside (see Read Before Heating!, page 25).

Coat one side of each piece of cheese with the brown sugar. Press the sugar into an even layer.

Remove the warm block (still on its baking sheet) from the oven and put the cheese, sugar side up, on the block. Return to the oven until the cheese is just beginning to go soft and the sugar melts, about 15 minutes.

Meanwhile, mix the oil, vinegar, and garlic together in a small bowl.

When the cheese is ready, remove the salt block setup from the oven. Toss the arugula with half of the dressing and make two mounds of greens on the block. Top each mound with the pear slices.

If you have a kitchen torch and you want to crisp the sugar a bit more, you may run a flame over it until the sugar bubbles and browns, about 10 seconds.

To serve, you may either smear the cheese onto toast or on the pear slices. Either way, top each bite with a small forkful of the wilted arugula.

Salt-Melted Chocolate Fondue with Crisp Bacon

There is only one reason why you don't eat chocolate fondue several times a week: It's a pain. Double boilers, pans to clean, burned bits at the bottom of your fondue pot, Sterno cans running out, drying out, leaking. Sure, liquid chocolate ecstasy is something we could all use more or less intravenously, but who needs the aggravation? Making fondue in a salt bowl is so much more convenient, so technically superior, that you will find yourself making it way more often. The bowl is thermally stable, so it acts like a double boiler, allowing you to make it in the same bowl you serve it in, and it will stay warm and delicious for hours. We'll add a few dashes of orange bitters to fruit things up. Dip into it with bacon (strawberries, bananas, graham crackers, and pretzels are also good) in order to better represent the food groups, and now there really is no reason why chocolate fondue can't be a mainstay for your household.

1 (1- to 2-cup) salt bowl

¼ cup heavy cream

8 to 12 pieces (8 to 12 ounces) thick-sliced bacon, cut into thirds

2 teaspoons orange bitters

1 cup bittersweet chocolate chips (64% cacao or higher)

MAKES 4 SERVINGS

Place the salt bowl on a burner over very low heat to warm to about 125°F, about 30 minutes (see Read Before Heating!, page 25). The bowl should feel just hot to the touch. If your burner doesn't go low enough, or you are using an electric burner, use a heat diffuser.

At the same time you set the bowl over the burner, remove the cream from the refrigerator to lose its chill.

Meanwhile, cook the bacon in a skillet over medium heat until crisp. Remove from the pan using a slotted spoon and place on paper towels to absorb excess fat and keep warm.

When ready to serve, put the cream in the salt bowl and warm for 1 minute. Remove from the heat. Add the bitters and chocolate chips and stir until everything is melted and smooth. Serve the warm bowl of chocolate fondue with the bacon strips for dipping.

Bagna Cauda Warmed in a Salt Bowl, Served with Artichokes

The American Midwest has hot dish, with its disconcertingly ambiguous name. Italians have "hot dip," or bagna cauda, which doesn't sound disconcerting because it sounds Italian. Both are essentially a hodgepodge of ingredients combined and served hot, but while the former is a deeply pragmatic affair, the latter is all about celebration. Preparing the bagna cauda in a salt bowl lends a striking salinity to the dish that first unifies and then time-warps the flavors to another plane. If this isn't enough, it amplifies it progressively, each bite you take sizzling with more clarity and exuberance. You don't need to know exactly what bagna cauda means, but, when served in a salt bowl, there's nothing ambiguous about it.

1 (1- to 2-cup) salt bowl

3 globe artichokes, trimmed

1 cup extra-virgin olive oil

20 garlic cloves, minced

4 ounces (1 stick) unsalted butter, cut into small pieces

10 anchovy fillets, finely chopped

1 teaspoon fresh lemon juice

Freshly ground black pepper

Pinch of cayenne pepper

½ baguette, cut into cubes or slices

MAKES 6 SERVINGS

Place the salt bowl on a burner over very low heat to warm to about 200°F, about 30 minutes (see Read Before Heating!, page 25). If your burner doesn't go low enough, or you are using an electric burner, use a heat diffuser.

Meanwhile, boil or steam the artichokes until the flesh at the base of the leaves is tender, about 30 minutes. Drain, cut in half lengthwise, scoop out the choke, and cut each half in half lengthwise; keep warm.

To make the bagna cauda, add ¼ cup of the olive oil and the garlic to the salt bowl and warm the mixture, stirring occasionally, until the aroma of garlic is intoxicating, about 4 minutes. Add the remaining ¾ cup oil and the butter. Stir until the butter is melted.

Stir in the anchovies and keep stirring and mashing until they dissolve, about 8 minutes. Stir in the lemon juice, black pepper, and cayenne.

Using two oven mitts, transfer the warm bowl of dip from the burner to the center of a heatproof ceramic platter and surround it with the artichoke quarters and bread cubes. Provide shrimp forks or skewers for dipping and a side bowl for the artichoke debris.

Salt Block Smashed Potatoes

Salt lovers have a tough time of it. We don't want to admit that we simply thrill to the taste of salted food; because salt is so primal, just talking about it makes us seem like compulsive maniacs. Eaters of sweets who can eat just three potato chips and then move on will never understand. Or will they? Smashing buttery potatoes down on a salt block is like making potato chips in surround sound, with big, thick, crispy skins warmed to salty, buttery perfection. There is nothing like it in the world, and if this doesn't unite us all as one smiling salty-sweet mass of humanity, I don't know what will.

1 (8- to 10-inch) square or (9-inch) round salt block

4 baking potatoes, about 8 ounces each

2 tablespoons unsalted butter

Freshly ground black pepper

MAKES 4 SERVINGS

Preheat the oven to 400°F. Bake the potatoes until the largest one can be pierced easily, about 45 minutes.

Meanwhile, put the salt block on a burner over low heat to warm to about 200°F, about 30 minutes (see Read Before Heating!, page 25). If your burner doesn't go low enough, or you are using an electric burner, use a heat diffuser.

When the potatoes are fully baked, remove from the oven and cut into quarters. Working with one potato at a time, lay the quarters, skin side down, on the block. Put a portion of butter on each potato quarter and season liberally with pepper. Use a knife to chop and smash the potato, still in its skin, scraping it up off the block as it breaks apart. When the potato is roughed up good, put it in a serving bowl. Smash the other potatoes in the same way.

Salt Block Raclette with Fire-Roasted New Potatoes and Shallots

Raclette was born to run. French shepherds shivering in the Alpine cold would hang the cheese from the hearth and hunker down literally inside the fireplaces, stropping the cheese onto hot potatoes as it melted. This recipe revels in the smoky rusticity of the original dish, but the introduction of a nice warm salt block lets you enjoy it at the dining room table instead of inside the gaping maw of a medieval fireplace.

1 (8- to 10-inch) square or (9-inch) round salt block

24 small new potatoes (red, golden, or fingerling)

1 tablespoon mild vegetable oil, such as canola

Freshly ground black pepper

12 shallots, unpeeled

12 cornichons (small pickled gherkins)

1 cup pickled vegetables, giardiniera, or Quick-Cured Vegetable Pickles (page 72)

1 pound raclette cheese, rind removed, cut into 2 thick slices

Paprika, for sprinkling

1 small baguette, sliced

MAKES 4 SERVINGS

Light a charcoal or wood fire to medium-low heat (see page 29). Leave the grill grate off the grill so the coals are accessible.

Put the salt block near the edge (the cooler part) of the fire (see Read Before Heating!, page 25). After 10 minutes, move the block into a hotter part of the fire. If you have heavy fireproof grill mitts (see page 21), it's easy (and oh-so-manly) to grab the block and move it with your hands. You can also use two sturdy metal spatulas to lift and move the block.

While the block is heating, coat the potatoes with the oil and season liberally with pepper. Wrap individually in small squares of heavy-duty aluminum foil. Put the potatoes directly in the coals and cook until they can be easily pierced with a fork, about 20 minutes, turning once or twice.

About 5 minutes before the potatoes are done, scatter the shallots in the coals and cook until the skins are charred, turning several times, about 5 minutes.

Using long-handled tongs or heavy grill gloves, transfer the potatoes and shallots to a large heat-proof serving platter or board. Put the salt block on the platter and scatter the cornichons and pickled vegetables around the salt block on the platter.

Put the slices of cheese on the block and cook until melted and brown on the edges. Flip the cheese with a sturdy spatula.

To serve, sprinkle the cheese with paprika. Portion out 6 potatoes and 3 shallots per person. Scrape some cheese over the top of each serving, being sure to include some of the browned edges. People may help themselves to the pickles. Serve with the baguette.

CHAPTER 4

COOKING ON (AND UNDER) SALT BLOCKS

Salt Brick Grilled Chicken

Salt-Fried Molasses Duck Breast with Scallion Pancakes and Espresso Hoisin

Salt Block Pressed Veal Paillard with Black Garlic Puree and Sage

Salt Block Cheesesteaks

Salt-Grilled Cheeseburger Sliders

Salt Block Beef Fajitas

Salt Block Seared Kobe Beef with Tarragon-Shallot Butter

Salt-Grilled Peppered Pork Tenderloin

Salt-Seared Calf's Liver and Bacon

Salt-Crisped Whole Fish with Mint and Pickled Ginger

Salt Crust Scallops with Thai Lime Dipping Sauce

Salt Block Rosemary Potato Chips

Prawns Stir-Seared with Hot Aromatic Salt Rocks

Salt-Cooked Chanterelle Frittata

Salt-Baked Johnnycakes

Salt Block Asparagus Rolled in Pancetta with Mostarda Dipping Sauce

Salt-Seared Sweet Potato Pancakes with Hot Pepper Honey

Salt-Roasted Poultry Gizzards Seasoned with Pastrami Pepper

Salt-Baked Walnut Brioche Scones

Salt-Seared Pineapple Steaks with Curried Agave Drizzle

Cinnamon Salt Plantains with Lemon-Espresso Syrup

Salt Crust Cardamom Naan

Salt-Griddled Blini with Sour Cream and Salt-Cured Candied Strawberries

Salt-Baked Rustic Apple-Onion Tart with Blue Cheese

Salt Block Baked Pretzel Rolls with Mustard Butter

Salt-Baked Chocolate Chip–Oatmeal Whoppers

Heat cooks and so does salt. What makes cooking on salt so cool is that heat and salt each get a chance to cook in their own way. Heat cooks by putting energy into food, firming proteins, melting fats, swelling starches, and making aromatic flavors bloom.

Salt cooks in an entirely different way, via chemical reactions. Moisture from the food dissolves the salt into its constituent ions—sodium, magnesium, calcium, chloride, carbonate, and so forth. These ions go to work breaking down the molecules in food. Complex proteins are broken down into amino acids, increasing flavor and tenderizing texture, so prawns tossed onto a bed of hot rock salt (see page 139) taste richer and more complex, and feel plumper to the bite. Salt also lowers the gelation temperature of starches, making them swell and soften sooner. This can be a subtle thing with sweet potato pancakes (see page 148) or an arresting thing with rosemary potato chips (see page 137).

Both salt and heat draw water out of food, concentrating the flavor and firming textures, but where heat does it by constricting proteins, wringing moisture out like a sponge, salt does it by gently pulling the moisture out of cells. What fire does by brute force, salt accomplishes with delicate diplomacy. Together, salt and heat play good cop/bad cop with your food—and they get results. Seared calf's liver (see page 130) comes off a block moister, less gamey, and with a better sear, while beef fajitas (see page 123) seared on a salt block taste, quite simply, huge, while the meat stays wonderfully tender.

The five fundamentals for cooking on a salt block are moisture, time, temperature, thickness, and fat. The moisture in the food is what dissolves the salt of the salt block and frees it to intermingle with the food. Foods with less available moisture, like asparagus wrapped in pancetta (see page 145) or a rustic apple-onion tart (see page 163), dissolve less salt and dissolve it more slowly, and thus will be seasoned less as they cook. These dryer foods can cook on a salt block for a longer time without acquiring too much salt. Foods with lots of available moisture, like a roasted whole fish (see page 131) or johnnycakes (see page 144), will dissolve more water faster and will take on more salt more rapidly. Really moist foods, like tomatoes, can only be cooked briefly before they take on a lot of salt.

Heat changes this dynamic. A blazing-hot salt block will dry the surface of most ingredients so quickly that salt-dissolving juices are kept at bay, at least for a few minutes. If the block is hot enough, even very moist foods like scallops (see page 134) will sear before they have a chance to dissolve much salt, though the salt makes them irresistibly firm and buttery. The golden crust that is formed then provides a protective bed on which the food can cook without being salted further. Heat is deceptive because while it accelerates the cooking process, it can slow down the salting process.

This is not to say that everything you cook on a salt block has to be socked with a white-hot sear for fear of salting your snack into oblivion. Sometimes slower cooking of a moister food can be exactly what you are looking for. Thicker foods like a big fat roasted pork tenderloin (see page 128) can cook on a salt block for a good 45 minutes and deliver perfect results. This is because while the surface of the meat may get heavily seasoned, the interior remains relatively salt-free. When sliced up, the salt from the skin commingles with the interior juices on your plate. The seasoning varies slightly from one piece to the next, humming melodically with every bite.

And don't forget this last helpful set of facts: Salt is not fat soluble; and water and fat don't like to mix. No matter how long oil rests or cooks on a salt block, it will not take up any salt. This means that fat rendered from the food onto the salt block forms a protective layer that keeps the food's foodiness and the salt's saltiness to themselves. Salt-Fried Molasses Duck Breast (see page 113) is a case in point: You will never taste a more perfectly cooked or seasoned duck breast.

Pouring or brushing a little oil onto your hot salt block partially converts it to a frying pan, letting the oil convect energy from the block to the food without the foods moisture having a say in the matter. Also, because oil and salt don't mix well, the oil frustrates the attempts of the food's liquids to reach the salt in the block. Whether you are cooking something burly like cheeseburger sliders (see page 121) or something elegant like warm salad with seared gizzards (see page 150), think of fat as the stern chaperone who keeps wetness and salt discreetly separated, resulting in dishes with a mild, G-rated saltiness.

Which brings us to another unique property of the salt block: its indubitable heft. Turn that hot, heavy salt block upside down and set it on *pollo al mattone*, chicken grilled under a brick (see page 111). This is the poultry equivalent of a panini. The compact, sinful texture you get from chicken nuggets with massive countryside flavor is like the best char-grilled Tuscan barbecue.

Every time you cook a food, consider its moistness, how long you think it will need to cook, how hot you want to cook it, the thickness of the food, and whether or not fat should be or is a part of the equation. It sounds a little intimidating, but looking at a specific food quickly simplifies it. Bacon shouldn't be cooked on too hot a surface and also it should be cut thin. But it is super fatty, so it can cook on a block for quite a while and come out barely salted. Shrimp has moderate moisture. It has no fat of its own, but it cooks so fast that it will come out perfectly salted no matter what you do. That's the beauty: Cooking on salt blocks is easy and intuitive.

Cooking with salt blocks does require some special attention. Proper hand protection is required, and using the right tools is essential for getting the best results. Read the sections titled Read Before Heating! (see page 25) and Utensils and Gear (see page 21) before proceeding to any of the recipes that follow. The process for heating salt blocks is specific to the heat source. Follow the instructions for heating on gas versus electric ranges (see page 28), for heating salt bowls (see page 25), for tempering and heating blocks in ovens (see page 30), and for cooking on gas or coal grills (see page 29). Every time you cook on a salt block, and especially the first time you heat a new salt block, review the cautions and disclaimers on page 25.

Follow the recommended best practices and salt blocks can safely, routinely, and enjoyably be heated up in excess of 600°F time and time again. Be sure to treat your salt block with respect, keeping in mind the fact that it is the unfathomable crystalline soul of an ocean that vanished long before hungry land-based organisms such as yourself were even a glimmer in a mother's eye.

BEST PRACTICES: 9 CARDINAL RULES FOR SALT BLOCK COOKING SUCCESS

1 Heat cookware grade salt blocks only.
2 Heat them slowly.
3 Temper blocks if using oven.
4 Use proper hand protection and tools.
5 Sear the moist.
6 Sizzle the fatty.
7 Take your time with the thick.
8 Cool before cleaning.
9 Scrub and sponge damp, not wet.

Salt Brick Grilled Chicken

Pollo al mattone is more soulful and elegant than its name—chicken grilled under a brick (a mattone is a heavy tile)—would lead you to imagine. Plain and delicious, with crisp skin and juicy meat, the dish is a staple of Tuscan cooking. Chicken halves are weighted as they grill, which brings the skin of the bird more uniformly in contact with the fire. Dehydration crisps the surface, but the center remains moist. A simple switcheroo reinvents and improves upon the traditional recipe's quiet genius. By replacing the brick with a block of salt, you add a new dimension of seasoning and even increase the crisping—a second Tuscan Renaissance.

2 (4 by 8 by 2-inch) salt blocks

1 (4-pound) chicken, preferably free-range

2 tablespoons olive oil

4 garlic cloves, halved lengthwise

½ teaspoon coarsely ground black pepper

Juice of ½ lemon

MAKES 4 SERVINGS

Place the salt blocks on a grill grate of a gas grill over low heat, close the lid, and warm for 10 minutes (see Read Before Heating!, page 25) while you prepare the chicken. Turn the heat to medium and heat the block for 10 more minutes. Its surface should be about 375°F (see Getting It Hot, page 24). If you are using a charcoal fire, set up a bilevel fire with half the grill set up for low heat (one layer of coals) and the other half set up for medium heat (two layers of coals).

Remove and discard the neck and package of innards from the cavity of the chicken. Place the chicken, breast side down, on a cutting board. With a large knife or poultry shears, cut down the length of the spine on both sides. Remove the spine. Cut the breast side of the chicken in half lengthwise. You will now have two chicken halves.

Wash the halves in cold water and pat dry with paper towels. Coat with the olive oil and rub all over with the cut sides of the garlic cloves; afterward tuck the pieces of garlic under the edges of the skin. Season all over with the pepper.

Clean the area of the grill grate not occupied by the salt block with a wire brush. Put the chicken halves, skin side down, on the grill grate and, using grill gloves or thick oven mitts, put a hot salt block on top of each half. Close the lid and cook until the chicken skin is crisp and deeply grill-marked, about 15 minutes.

Remove the blocks using the grill gloves, flip the chicken halves with tongs, put the blocks back on top of the chicken, close the lid, and cook until an instant-read thermometer inserted into the inside of the thicker thigh registers 170°F, 10 to 15 minutes.

Remove the salt blocks, transfer the chicken to a clean cutting board, and let rest for 5 minutes before cutting into parts. Drizzle with the lemon juice and serve.

Salt-Fried Molasses Duck Breast with Scallion Pancakes and Espresso Hoisin

The farm in the south of France where I lived for a few years raised the best duck I have ever encountered. The animals were an esteemed breed from the region, the feed was obsessively sourced from a local grower, the water was always fresh from a well, and the straw in their coop was kept so clean you could make a bed of it. My favorite way to prepare duck breast was the simplest: Salt the magret and toss it onto a heavy tile of black slate shimmering with heat among the coals of an open fire. Nothing could ever touch that—until I discovered salt blocks, which simplify and improve the technique by using a simple salt block instead of salt and slate. Add to that a little inspiration from the French-influenced flavors of Southeast Asia and who knows where your mouth will transport you?

1 (8- to 10-inch) shallow salt dish (not a flat salt block)

Duck

1 (1-pound) skin-on duck breast

2 tablespoons molasses

Finely grated zest and juice of ½ lemon

Sauce

2 tablespoons finely ground dark roasted coffee

¼ cup boiling water

3 tablespoons hoisin sauce

1 teaspoon molasses

Pancakes

1 cup unbleached all-purpose flour

½ cup boiling water

2 tablespoons toasted sesame oil

½ cup thinly sliced scallion greens

Pinch of crushed red pepper flakes

MAKES 2 SERVINGS

NOTE: This recipe calls for a shallow, carved salt dish, but a flat salt block can also work. Use a paper towel to mop off the fat from the duck breast as it renders. Use store-bought duck fat or vegetable oil to fry the scallion pancakes.

To make the duck, score the duck skin by cutting through the skin and the fat layer beneath it with a small sharp knife in a crisscross pattern. Mix the molasses, lemon zest, and lemon juice in a quart-size zipper-lock plastic bag. Put the duck breast in the bag and seal the bag, pushing out any excess air. Massage the marinade into the meat and refrigerate for at least 4 hours, or up to overnight.

To make the sauce, mix the coffee and boiling water; let sit for 5 minutes. Strain out the solids through a small fine-mesh strainer. Mix the resulting "coffee" with the hoisin and molasses; set aside until ready to serve.

To make the pancakes, mix the flour and boiling water into a soft pliable dough. Knead briefly on a clean work surface, just until the dough is smooth. Form the dough into a rough rectangle, wrap in plastic wrap, and let sit at room temperature for 30 minutes or overnight in the refrigerator.

Put the salt dish over low heat on the stovetop or gas grill for 10 minutes (see Read Before Heating!, page 25). Turn the heat to medium and heat the salt plate for 10 more minutes. Raise the heat to medium-high and heat the dish to about 450°F (see Getting It Hot, page 24).

Meanwhile, roll the pancake dough out on a floured board into a rectangle about ⅛ inch thick. Brush the top with the sesame oil and make a layer of the scallions over the surface; season with the red pepper flakes. Starting with one of the long sides, roll up the dough and scallions tightly, like a jelly roll. Cut the roll in half and spiral each piece into a circle. Flatten with your hands and then roll each circle gently into a 6-inch pancake; set aside.

Remove the duck breast from the marinade and pat dry. Discard the marinade.

Put the duck breast, fat side down, on the preheated salt dish and cook. Spoon the fat into a medium skillet as it renders from the breast. When the skin on the duck breast is golden and crisp (after about 8 minutes), spoon as much remaining fat from the dish as possible, and flip the breast, flesh side down. Cook until the center of the breast registers 150°F on an instant-read thermometer, about 5 more minutes. Using a metal spatula, remove the duck from the salt dish and let sit for 5 minutes.

Put the skillet with the duck fat over medium-high heat. Fry the pancakes in the hot fat until golden, a minute or two per side. Transfer to paper towels to absorb excess fat from the surface.

Slice the duck breast across the grain into ¼-inch strips. Cut the pancakes into wedges. Serve the sliced duck and sliced pancakes drizzled with the espresso hoisin sauce.

Salt Block Pressed Veal Paillard with Black Garlic Puree and Sage

Paillards are all about whacking things into categorical submission with a mallet, and about the dubious tenderness achieved by a thrashing. Salt blocks ask us to reject this patrician clubbing of our food in favor of something more interesting. A thin slice of veal sizzled between two hot salt blocks gives your mouth the unctuous texture we love in veal, with the fervent flavor that comes from cooking your food with salt and love. Add a little balsamic-simmered garlic to the mix and you'll forget all about the fun you could have had with that mallet.

2 (8- to 10-inch) square or (9-inch round) salt blocks, at least 1½ inches thick

1 head garlic, broken in cloves, peeled and minced

1 cup balsamic vinegar (red, not white)

¼ teaspoon freshly ground black pepper

2 tablespoons unsalted butter, softened

12 ounces veal cutlet (leg), sliced about ¼ inch thick

6 medium fresh sage leaves, slivered

MAKES 4 SERVINGS

Simmer the garlic and balsamic vinegar in a medium skillet over medium-high heat until the garlic is soft and the liquid has reduced to a glaze (about 3 tablespoons), about 4 minutes. Season with the pepper and scrape into a small bowl. Smash the garlic into a coarse paste with the back of a fork; let cool. Once it has cooled, work the butter into the garlic mixture until smooth; set aside.

Put the salt blocks over low heat on the stovetop for 10 minutes (see Read Before Heating!, page 25). Turn the heat to medium and heat the salt block for 10 more minutes. Raise the heat to medium-high and heat the blocks to about 450°F (see Getting It Hot, page 24).

Brush the veal slices on both sides with half of the garlic butter. Put half of the slices on one of the hot salt blocks. Turn off the heat under the second block. Using heavy oven mitts, lift the second block and place on top of the veal slices to weigh them down. Cook for 2 to 3 minutes, then lift the top block. The veal should be flattened and cooked through. Transfer with a spatula to a serving plate and repeat with the remaining veal slices. Set a small spoonful of the remaining garlic butter on each slice of veal, scatter the sage leaves over the top, and serve.

Salt Block Cheesesteaks

If sinking your teeth into a tender, meaty, cheesy, peppery bite of Philadelphia cheesesteak conjures any thought at all, it is this: feud. Whose is best, Pat's King of Steaks or Geno's Steaks? What cheese is best, American or provolone? Should there be peppers? What should the roll look like? Who has the right to a certain trademark crown and catchphrases, the owner of Pat's or the owner of a competitor (owned by the cousin of Pat's owner)? It's enough to make your head spin. Step outside the fray and simply up the ante, cooking your vegetables and steak on a salt block for an indisputably delicious mouthful every time.

2 (8- to 10-inch) square or (9-inch) round salt blocks

2 garlic cloves, minced

Leaves from 8 thyme sprigs

Leaves from 6 oregano sprigs

4 fresh basil leaves, finely chopped

½ cup extra-virgin olive oil

Freshly ground black pepper

4 (6-inch) sub rolls, split

1 large red bell pepper, stemmed, seeded, and cut into thin strips

½ medium red onion, halved, thinly sliced, and broken into strips

4 ounces white mushrooms, sliced

1 pound boneless beef top round, shaved for steak sandwiches

12 slices provolone (8 ounces)

MAKES 4 SERVINGS

Place the salt blocks over low heat on a gas grill or stovetop for 10 minutes (see Read Before Heating!, page 25). Turn the heat to medium and heat for 10 more minutes. Turn the heat to medium-high and heat the blocks to about 500°F (see Getting It Hot, page 24).

Meanwhile, combine the garlic, thyme, oregano, basil, olive oil, and pepper in a medium bowl. Brush the interior of the rolls with a thin film of the oil mixture; set aside. Scrape half of the remaining oil mixture into another bowl and toss with the bell pepper, onion, and mushrooms. Toss the beef in a separate bowl with the other half of the remaining oil mixture.

Dump the vegetables and their oil onto the hot salt blocks and cook until the vegetables are barely tender, turning them frequently with a thin-blade slotted spatula, about 3 minutes. Transfer to a bowl.

Close the grill and allow the blocks to regain temperature, about 5 minutes.

Put the steak on the hot blocks and cook until it loses its raw look, turning with a spatula once or twice, about 3 minutes. Divide the steak into 4 piles; top each pile with 3 slices of cheese. Close the lid and cook until the cheese melts, about 30 seconds. Using a spatula, fill each roll with one of the piles of cheesesteak. Top with a portion of the vegetables and serve immediately.

Salt-Grilled Cheeseburger Sliders

Sitting on a curb in St. Paul, Minnesota, as a youth after canoeing through the glaciated lakelands up north, my mind hummed like a newly forged brass bell. My heart was pure, open, my body clean and sinewy and brown, and my mind untethered, wandering the constellations. But three weeks of subsisting on burnt fish (always so hungry, we'd throw gutted fish straight into the fire), hardtack, and invincible government-issue processed cheese does not provoke dreams of chaste spirituality. They converge into a singular impure thought: burger! Staring at the wet and iridescent city streets as blind humanity hurries by in shoes, I stuff my face from a ten-burger-deep bag of sliders that moments before sizzled on a griddle. Replace that griddle with a white-hot block of salt and the sliders develop great depths of flavor even as they brown from the heat. Salt block sliders are enlightenment you can sink your teeth into.

2 (8- to 10-inch) square or (9-inch) round salt blocks

2 pounds ground beef (85% to 95% lean)

¼ cup milk

3 tablespoons ketchup

1½ tablespoons brown mustard

1 teaspoon freshly ground black pepper

Vegetable oil, to coat burgers and blocks

3 ounces cheddar, cut into 3 slices, each slice quartered

12 small soft rolls, split

2 medium tomatoes, each cut into 6 slices

MAKES 6 SERVINGS

Place the salt blocks over low heat on a gas grill for 10 minutes (see Read Before Heating!, page 25). Turn the heat to medium and heat for 10 more minutes. Turn the heat to medium-high and heat the blocks to about 500°F (see Getting It Hot, page 24).

Meanwhile, mix the ground beef with the milk, ketchup, mustard, and pepper. Form into 12 meatballs. Flatten into patties between your hands. Pinch the center of each burger, forming a 1-inch-wide dimple. As the burgers cook, these indents will fill in, and the finished burgers will be beautifully flat rather than bulging. Coat the burgers thoroughly with oil.

Carefully brush the hot salt blocks with oil. Grill the burgers on both sides until browned and resilient, about 3 minutes per side. Put a cheese slice on each burger. When the cheese melts, after about 30 seconds, transfer the burgers with a spatula to a clean baking sheet.

Open the rolls, place on the salt blocks, cut side down, and toast until browned, about 1 minute. Put a burger on each toasted roll and top with a tomato slice. Serve immediately.

Salt Block Beef Fajitas

The day you buy your first salt block, grab some skirt steak from a Mexican market on the way home; fire up the grill; throw the salt block, some chiles and tortillas, and the steak on the grill; and stand around with family making fajitas to order, cutting pieces of meat right off the block. Thirty minutes later the kids will be off on skateboards and you'll be wandering into the kitchen in search of a cold beer with which to ice your singed fingers. It'll be months before it even occurs to you to refine the vaquero simplicity to the point where you can actually invite people over and feed them a civilized meal. When you're there, try this recipe with marinated chicken, or shrimp, or rockfish. Just don't fuss, enjoy the moment, and wear a cowboy hat while you cook.

1 (8- to 10-inch) square or (9-inch) round salt block

1 tablespoon smoked sweet paprika

2 teaspoons ground toasted cumin

1 teaspoon ground chipotle chile

2 teaspoons dried oregano

½ teaspoon freshly ground black pepper

2 garlic cloves, minced

2 pounds beef skirt steak or flank steak

1 large Spanish onion, cut into slices about ½ inch thick

1 large red onion, cut into slices about ½ inch thick

1 tablespoon canola oil

1 green poblano chile

1 red bell pepper

8 (8- or 10-inch) flour tortillas

4 lime wedges, for serving

2 cups salsa of your choice

¾ cup sour cream (optional)

MAKES 4 TO 8 SERVINGS

Mix the paprika, cumin, chipotle chile, oregano, black pepper, and garlic in a large bowl. Slice the beef against its grain into ¼-inch-thick slices. Dredge the beef strips in the spice mix. Refrigerate for at least 2 hours, or up to 24 hours.

When ready to grill, place the salt block over low heat on a gas grill set up for bilevel cooking for 10 minutes (see Read Before Heating!, page 25). If you are using gas, turn the heat to medium and heat for 10 more minutes. If you are using charcoal, move the salt block toward the hotter part of the fire. If you are using gas, raise the heat to high and heat the block to about 550°F (see Getting It Hot, page 24). If you are using charcoal, move the block directly over the hottest part of the fire.

While the block is heating, brush the onion slices with the oil.

Once the grill is hot, you can grill the chile pepper, bell pepper, and onions on the area of the grill grate around the block. Put the whole peppers on the grill, close the lid, and grill until blackened on all sides, about 10 minutes. Remove the peppers from the grill, put them in a paper bag, and set aside for 10 minutes to cool. Stem and seed the peppers and cut into strips; keep warm.

Grill the onion slices until grill-marked and just starting to become tender, about 5 minutes, flipping them gently halfway through. Wrap in aluminum foil and keep warm.

Grill the tortillas on the grill grate until they are spotted with char marks, about 2 minutes per side. Wrap in foil and keep warm.

Cook the beef strips on the hot salt block, about 12 strips at a time. Cook just until seared on both sides, about 20 seconds per side. Transfer to a serving platter and keep warm; repeat with the remaining strips.

Arrange the pepper strips, onions, and lime wedges around the beef on the platter. Serve with the warm tortillas, salsa, and sour cream on the side. Allow guests to roll up the beef, peppers, and onions in the tortillas with the salsa, sour cream, and a squeeze of lime.

Salt Block Seared Kobe Beef with Tarragon-Shallot Butter

Dress yourself to cook this dish. White button-down shirt, cuff links, seersucker, bow tie, silk kerchief, silk socks, saddle shoes. Greet your guests at the door with a kiss for the women and a firm handshake for the men. Pour a round of good martinis for all. This is the true classic of salt block cookery. Superbly marbleized meat struck with a flash of salty heat, with a little butter for panache. You are the picture of genteel hosting, graciously, effortlessly, unquestioningly taking care of the serious business of celebrating life.

1 (8- to 10-inch) square or (9-inch) round salt block

12 ounces trimmed boneless Kobe beef loin

2 shallots, finely chopped

¼ cup dry vermouth

Leaves from 1 tarragon sprig, coarsely chopped

Freshly ground coarse black pepper

3 tablespoons unsalted butter, softened

MAKES 2 SERVINGS

Place the salt block over low heat on a gas grill or a stovetop for 10 minutes (see Read Before Heating!, page 25). Turn the heat to medium and heat for 10 more minutes. Raise the heat to high and heat the block to about 550°F (see Getting It Hot, page 24).

While the block is heating, put the beef in the freezer for 15 minutes to firm it. Do not allow it to freeze.

Meanwhile, combine the shallots and vermouth in a medium skillet over medium-high heat and boil until only 1 tablespoon of the vermouth remains in the pan. Stir frequently to make sure the shallots do not boil dry. Stir in the tarragon and pepper. Let cool to room temperature. Mix the shallots into the butter and set aside.

Remove the beef from the freezer and slice against the grain into ¼-inch-thick slices.

Just before serving, make sure the block is up to temperature, and then sear the beef, a few pieces at a time, for about 30 seconds per side. Serve in a tangle topped with spoonfuls of the tarragon-shallot butter.

SALT BLOCK YOUR STEAK

The debate about how to salt a steak has raged since the invention of salt and steak. Grilling the meat au naturel, then serving it with a flourish of finishing salt, produces a dazzling interplay of salt and savoriness in the mouth but does not always fully develop the flavors of the meat. Sprinkling the steak with salt 20 to 30 minutes ahead of time helps to build flavor and develop a crust, but can be monotonous, with each bite identical to the last. It can also easily result in a steak that is overseasoned or dried out.

Here's a new idea to fuel the food fight. Let a raw steak stand on a salt block for 20 minutes before cooking it. This draws out just enough moisture to help develop a delicious crust, but no more. Because the solid slab of salt dissolves much more slowly than granular salt, the seasoning releases slowly, giving it time to penetrate gradually, without becoming overseasoned. And because the steak is in full contact with the salt, it develops flavor across every square millimeter of its surface. Pull your steak off the grill and sprinkle it with a little coarse, moist, mineral-rich salt like sel gris. Then decide for yourself: Is it the best steak you've ever eaten, or is it merely awesome?

Salt-Grilled Peppered Pork Tenderloin

Sanlúcar de Barrameda, in the south of Spain, is famous for its sherry. But what I remember about the place is a huge old mill that was transformed into a restaurant. Burly mustachioed Spaniards flung giant slabs of beef, pork, and sausage onto a flaming grill and served them up under a mountain of fries. We took our food and a pitcher of chilled red wine back to benches that stretched into the smoky distance of the hangar and dug in. The clean fresh flavor of lime, the piquant pizzazz of the pepper, and beautifully pink, buttery soft flesh beneath the enticingly thin and crispy crust of this tenderloin tastes like the memory of a great food discovery.

2 (8- to 10-inch) square salt blocks

1 tablespoon finely cracked black peppercorns

1 garlic clove, minced

3 juniper berries, finely chopped

3 tablespoons plus 2 teaspoons extra-virgin olive oil

1 (1¾-pound) pork tenderloin

Zest and juice of ½ lime

MAKES 4 SERVINGS

Mix the cracked peppercorns, garlic, juniper berries, and 3 tablespoons of the olive oil in a small bowl.

Butterfly the pork loin by slitting the meat lengthwise, leaving it attached along one side. Open the meat like a book. It should be no more than 2 inches thick. Rub the pork all over with the spice mixture and set aside for about 1 hour.

Meanwhile, put the salt blocks over low heat on the grate of a gas grill for 10 minutes (see Read Before Heating!, page 25). Turn the heat to medium and heat for 10 more minutes. Raise the heat to medium-high and heat the blocks to about 450°F (see Getting It Hot, page 24).

Put the pork on the hot salt blocks and cook until the meat is browned on both sides and resilient but not firm, about 5 minutes per side. A thermometer inserted in a thicker part of the pork should register 140°F. Transfer the pork to a cutting board and let it rest for 10 minutes before slicing.

Cut the pork crosswise in ¼-inch-thick slices and shingle on a platter. Scatter the lime zest over the slices and drizzle with lime juice and the remaining 2 teaspoons olive oil and serve immediately.

Salt-Seared Calf's Liver and Bacon

"He liked thick giblet soup, nutty gizzards, a stuffed roast heart, liver slices fried with crust-crumbs. . . ." Never was there a better liver lover than the blissfully dull Leopold Bloom, who wandered James Joyce's Dublin in the most transcendentally normal day ever attempted in literature. Liver is so unexceptionally ordinary that we tend to forget its exciting, oddly primal tang. But the remedy for calf's liver boredom is not Bloom's "crustcrumbs." Instead, sear each side on a salt block with a little bacon fat. One bite will ignite in your taste buds the same feral spark that kindled Bloom's wife to literature's most ecstatic soliloquy.

1 (8- to 10-inch) square or (9-inch) round salt block

12 ounces calf's liver, in 4 (¼-inch-thick) slices

Freshly ground black pepper

1 piece thick-sliced bacon, quartered

1 tablespoon sherry vinegar

1 tablespoon finely chopped fresh flat-leaf parsley

MAKES 2 SERVINGS

Place the salt block over low heat on a gas grill or stovetop for 10 minutes (see Read Before Heating!, page 25). Turn the heat to medium and heat for 10 more minutes. Raise the heat to medium-high and heat the block to about 450°F (see Getting It Hot, page 24).

While the block is heating, trim thick pieces of membrane from the liver slices, and season both sides with pepper.

Put the bacon on the salt block and cook until crisp. If bacon fat starts dripping off the sides of the block, mop as needed with a folded paper towel. Be careful not to burn yourself; the fat is hot. Remove the bacon from the block and reserve.

Put the liver slices on the hot block and cook just until seared on both sides, about 1 minute per side.

Transfer the liver to two plates. Drizzle each portion with the vinegar and top each with two pieces of bacon and half the parsley; serve immediately.

Salt-Crisped Whole Fish with Mint and Pickled Ginger

How do you get kids to jump into the station wagon when going out for sushi? For every bite you want them to eat, "to broaden their horizons," give them a salty-crispy chunk of fried salmon skin. I haven't a clue what the sushi does for their "horizons," but it will convince them of the necessity of crispy-chewy fish skin. Broiling on a hot salt block firms, cooks, and crisps a fish beautifully, making eating a simple pleasure for the whole family.

1 (8 by 12-inch or larger) salt block

2 tablespoons packed pickled ginger slices for sushi, finely chopped

1 garlic clove, minced

Leaves from 4 large mint sprigs

2 teaspoons toasted sesame oil

Sea salt and freshly ground black pepper

2 whole fish (about 1½ pounds each) with delicious skin, such as red snapper, pompano, striped bass, etc.

Juice and zest of 1 large lime

MAKES 4 SERVINGS

Place the salt block over low heat on a gas grill or stovetop for 10 minutes (see Read Before Heating!, page 25). Turn the heat to medium and heat for 10 more minutes. Raise the heat to medium-high and heat the block to about 500°F, about 10 more minutes. For the last 10 minutes, also preheat the oven to 500°F (see Getting It Hot, page 24).

Meanwhile, mix the ginger, garlic, mint, and 1 teaspoon of the oil. Season with salt and pepper. Cut three diagonal slices in the sides of both fish. Fill each slit with 1 teaspoon of the ginger mixture. Pack the rest into the fishes' cavities. Rub the remaining 1 teaspoon oil all over the fish.

Using two heavy oven mitts, transfer the block to a baking sheet. Put the fish on the hot block and slip the pan into the preheated oven. Roast for 5 minutes, then turn over with a metal spatula, scraping carefully to avoid tearing the skin, and roast until the flesh of the fish flakes to gentle pressure, about 5 more minutes.

Transfer the fish to a serving platter using a wide spatula. Scatter the lime zest over the fish and drizzle with the lime juice. Serve, removing the fish from the bone at the table (see Serving Whole Fish).

SERVING WHOLE FISH

Make a slit through the skin of the cooked fish down the length of the spine right above the dorsal fin, using a narrow knife. Insert a spatula into the slit and slide it between the flesh and the bone. Make a slice just behind the head and just in front of the tail, separating the top fillet from the skeleton. Lift the released fillet from the carcass and serve.

Using the spatula or two forks, lift the central skeleton, including the head and the tail, from the bottom fillet and discard. Serve the bottom fillet.

Salt Crust Scallops
with Thai Lime Dipping Sauce

A famous direction given to bartenders by drinkers of the dry Martini cocktail is, "just wave the bottle of vermouth over the gin." The conceit is that gin chilled over ice and strained is pretty dang good, and that the addition of the vermouth will only diminish it. Fresh scallops are pretty much the same as gin in this regard, and any attempt to improve on their plump, firm, buttery perfection risks resulting in the opposite. In both cases, this notion is pretty and witty, but it is not wise. Vermouth is what makes a good Martini the touchstone of bartending. A scallop salt-seared to crispy golden perfection turns a nice bite into spellbinding bliss. Doused in sesame-citrus sauce, it is the new benchmark in cooking shellfish.

1 (9- to 10-inch) square salt block

¼ cup fresh lime juice

¼ cup Thai fish sauce

1 tablespoon rice wine vinegar

2 tablespoons toasted sesame oil

1 garlic clove, minced

1 hot chile pepper, such as bird chile, habanero, cayenne, or Scotch bonnet, stem and seeds removed, minced

¼ cup finely shredded carrot

1¼ pounds large wild-caught sea scallops (about 16)

½ teaspoon freshly ground black pepper

MAKES 4 SERVINGS

Place the salt block over low heat on a gas grill or stovetop for 10 minutes (see Read Before Heating!, page 25). Turn the heat to medium and heat for 10 more minutes. Raise the heat to medium-high and heat the block to about 600°F, about 20 more minutes (see Getting It Hot, page 24).

To make the dipping sauce, mix the lime juice, fish sauce, ¼ cup water, vinegar, sesame oil, garlic, chile pepper, and carrot; set aside.

Pat the scallops dry and pull off their white gristly tendons if not already removed. Season the scallops with the black pepper and let stand at room temperature until the salt block is hot.

When the salt block is very hot (you should only be able to hold your hand above it for just a few seconds), place the scallops on the hot block and sear until browned and springy to the touch but still a little soft in the center, about 3 minutes per side. Work in batches if your salt block cannot comfortably fit all the scallops at once.

Transfer to a platter or plates and serve with the dipping sauce.

Salt Block Rosemary Potato Chips

It's amazing what you can do with a little love, a little labor, and a salt block. Foods that you might consider junk food in the supermarket become flat-out delicacies at home. Sizzling through the mantis green sheen of olive oil, the salt block lends the potato enough salt to bring its addictive starchy flavor alive but not so much that it distracts from the pungent rosemary. The potato chips taste like what they are: a fresh vegetable crisped and seasoned to perfection.

1 (8- to 10-inch) square or (9-inch) round salt block

2 medium round potatoes, thinly sliced

3 tablespoons olive oil

½ teaspoon freshly ground black pepper

1 teaspoon coarsely chopped fresh rosemary leaves

MAKES 2 SERVINGS

Place the salt block on a stovetop burner over low heat for 10 minutes (see Read Before Heating!, page 25). Turn the heat to medium and heat for 10 more minutes. Raise the heat to medium-high and heat the block to about 450°F (see Getting It Hot, page 24).

While the block is heating, toss the potatoes with the olive oil, making sure that the oil coats all of the slices. Lay the slices on the hot block in a single layer. You should be able to fit about half the slices on the block at a time. Cook until browned on one side, about 5 minutes. Using a heavy metal spatula, lift each potato slice, scraping it from the salt to make sure you don't leave behind any part of the browned crusty skin. Season the flipped potatoes with half the pepper and rosemary. Brown the potato slices on the other side, about 4 more minutes. When browned and crisp, transfer to a serving bowl; cook the remaining slices in the same way. Serve immediately.

Prawns Stir-Seared with Hot Aromatic Salt Rocks

Scientists still argue over who used fire first: us, our hoary brethren the Neanderthals, or even our much earlier ancestors homo erectus. Who deserves the glory? The earliest evidence of controlled fire was found in South Africa's Wonderwerk Cave and dates to some 1 million years ago, but we likely learned about fire's capabilities from nature much earlier than that, foraging through the aftermath of a wildfire for the snakes, lizards, rodents, and other small animals that got cooked alive in the blaze. Yum! One thing is for sure: We human beings are crazy about cooking—my buddy, chef Vitaly Paley, followed this notion to its logical extreme, tossing a handful of whole critters into a scalding rubble of rock salt is a simple but elegant evocation of our earliest cuisine. Each big, buttery, bodacious bite will have you wondering, which species was it that first licked its fingers?

2 pounds Himalayan salt rocks, coarse salt, or broken salt blocks

12 black peppercorns, smashed with a hammer

4 cinnamon sticks, smashed with a hammer

4 star anise pods, broken into pieces

Large pinch of crushed red pepper flakes

2 pounds spot prawns, heads on

1 lime, cut lengthwise into 8 wedges

MAKE 4 SERVINGS

Preheat the oven to 400°F.

Mix the salt rocks, peppercorns, cinnamon, star anise, and red pepper flakes in a large nonreactive roasting pan. Heat in the oven for 40 minutes, until the salt is hot and the spices are aromatic.

Add the prawns and toss with the hot salt and cover for 10 minutes, until brightly colored and firm to the touch.

Remove the prawns from the salt mixture and serve with wedges of lime. Break the prawns in half at the head and peel the bodies with your fingers while you suck the heads with your mouth. If you've never sucked a prawn head before in your life, that day ends today.

FIFTEEN WAYS TO CELEBRATE
A BROKEN SALT BLOCK

A broken salt block is not a loss to be mourned, but rather it is an occasion to rejoice in new approaches to cooking and seasoning. Long before cooking on salt blocks became popular, freshly mined salt rocks were ground up to varying coarsenesses to serve the culinary needs of much of Asia. Whether you are grinding up your dearly departed salt blocks or simply starting with granular Himalayan pink salt from the store, the uniquely beautiful, smugly solid salt crystals invite you to explore new frontiers in cooking.

1 Using a stainless-steel grater, shave a salt block fragment into a fine powder over fatty fish and lean meat, or over dry foods such as nuts, popcorn, or candied apples.

2 Whack a chunk with a hammer and sprinkle fine shards over moist foods like lamb, squash, and curries, or use the shards to rim cocktail glasses.

3 Keep some on hand in a salt mill for opportunistic grinding at the table.

4 Sprinkle coarse grains on sauced foods for a lasting hard crunch.

5 Embed fragmented chunks in a pane of caramelized sugar to make salt brittle punctured by a stained glass glow of Gothic light.

6 Toss a chunk into water for cooking pasta or blanching vegetables.

7 Toss a chunk into your dishwasher and toss your packaged dish spot remover products out the window.

8 Put a bit in a jar of fruit preserves with a few pinches of each of your favorite Indian spices and convert sweet jam into savory chutney.

9 Leave a big chunk outside for the deer.

10 Serve pebbles or rocks of the salt as a garnish that dissolve into the seeping juices of a beef (or venison) steak as they swirl on the plate.

11 Make a Haiku with food:
chicken, green bean, salt rock
animal, vegetable, mineral

12 Become one with your salt block: If it's free of cooking odors, run a bath, drop in the block, and soak in your freshly reconstituted 600-million-year-old sea.

13 Save a well-proportioned fragment to use as a luminous butter dish at the dinner table.

14 Broil a whole fish on a bed of citrus and herbs and smashed-up broken salt brick.

15 Bash a big block to bits, heat it to blazing hot, and toss in some cockles, sea snails, and whole prawns to salt-cook your shellfish.

Salt-Cooked Chanterelle Frittata

Whomever invented cooking on a pan or griddle rather than on a grate or spit was on to something. Food gets browned but not charred, juices and stray tasty bits get eaten rather than simply falling into the fire, and miraculously, liquid foods can be cooked into solidity, so something once slurped through a straw can now be speared with a fork. Cooking a frittata on a salt block griddle embellishes the feat by creating a delicious salty crispy edge of flavor that celebrates the egg's transformation from viscous sip to unctuous bite. If only the inventor of the griddle had done a little digging, he or she might have really come up with something revolutionary.

1 (8- to 10-inch) square or (9-inch) round salt block

4 large or extra-large eggs

1 tablespoon milk

¼ teaspoon freshly ground black pepper

1 tablespoon olive oil, plus more for the rings

2 ounces chanterelle mushrooms, thinly sliced

2 scallions, trimmed and thinly sliced

MAKES 2 SERVINGS

Place the salt block over low heat on a stovetop burner for 10 minutes (see Read Before Heating!, page 25). Turn the heat to medium and heat for 10 more minutes. Raise the heat to medium-high and heat the block to about 400°F, 5 more minutes (see Getting It Hot, page 24).

Beat the eggs in a bowl until lightly airy. Mix in the milk and pepper; set aside.

Coat the surface of the hot block with the oil. Spread the chanterelles and scallions over the block and sauté until the mushrooms lose their raw look, scraping and tossing with a rigid metal spatula, about 3 minutes. Turn off the heat under the block.

Oil the interior of two egg rings or one 6-inch pastry ring. Surround the sautéed vegetables with the ring(s), and spread the vegetables out so that they are dispersed evenly in the ring(s). Pour the egg mixture into the ring(s). Cook until the bottom and sides of the egg mixture are set, about 2 minutes. Carefully remove the ring(s). Flip the frittata(s) with a metal spatula to cook the top side(s). Cook for 1 minute longer. Serve immediately.

NOTE: Using egg rings (or a pastry ring) helps keep the eggs from running over the edge of the block. However, as long as the block is good and hot, it is possible to cook without one. Pour the eggs slowly over the salt block with one hand, pushing back any tentacles of liquid egg as they roam. After a few seconds, the eggs will be firm enough to keep their shape.

Salt-Baked Johnnycakes

Johnnycakes are more quintessentially American than apple pie, if for no other reason than they reveal more about America's roots. Sometimes they're called Shawnee cakes, referring to their ties to the fried corn bread of Native Americans. They are also called journey cakes because they are, like matzo, an unleavened bread that can quickly be made while on the go. African-American slaves, who would cook them up while in the fields, right on their work tools, called them hoecakes. Given their storied past, baking johnnycakes on a salt block would barely qualify as remarkable were it not for their taste. The cakes' salt-glazed surfaces shine with the lightly sweetened corn flavor that is indisputably American.

1 (9- to 10-inch) square salt block

¾ cup unbleached all-purpose flour

¾ cup stone-ground cornmeal

1 tablespoon light brown sugar

½ teaspoon baking soda

Pinch of fine sea salt, such as
    fleur de sel

1 egg

1 cup buttermilk

1 tablespoon unsalted butter, melted

Vegetable oil, for coating the salt
    block

Maple syrup or Hot Pepper Honey
    (page 148), for serving

MAKES 4 SERVINGS

Place the salt block over low heat on a stovetop burner for 10 minutes (see Read Before Heating!, page 25). Turn the heat to medium and heat for 10 more minutes. Raise the heat to medium-high and heat the block to about 400°F, 5 more minutes (see Getting It Hot, page 24).

As soon as the block is hot, mix the flour, cornmeal, brown sugar, baking soda, and salt in a large bowl. Add the egg and buttermilk and mix just enough so that everything is moistened. Stir in the melted butter.

Coat the surface of the hot block with a thin film of oil. Spoon batter onto the hot block to make small pancakes, about 2 inches across each, leaving about 1 inch between them. Cook until crisp and brown on the bottom and set up at the sides, about 2 minutes. Flip with a spatula and cook on the other side until puffed and browned on the bottom. Transfer to a plate with a spatula and keep warm. Cook the remaining pancakes and serve with syrup.

Salt Block Asparagus Rolled in Pancetta with Mostarda Dipping Sauce

Put yourself in a Fiat convertible en route to a salumeria off in the countryside outside of Bologna. A woman with a lead foot and hair like spun sugar is shouting in Italian about salt and pig, and you are shielding your face from the wind-whipped frenzy of her hair. You tilt your head back and look straight up at the sky, and the music from the radio and the sun wrap you up and lift you away. Later that night, drinking a cold beer on a crowded piazza, you open your bag and wrap fresh figs and raw string beans and Parmesan cheese chunks in cured pork, all slathered in the revelation that is mustard oil–infused fruit preserves. I am there with her now. Fry your bacon-wrapped asparagus on a salt block and dip it in homemade mostarda, and you won't even wish you were there with us.

1 (8 to 10-inch) square or (9-inch) round salt block

2 tablespoons bitter orange marmalade

2 tablespoons mustard oil (available in Indian groceries)

Juice of ½ orange (2 to 3 tablespoons)

1 tablespoon chopped kalamata olives

1 tablespoon brown mustard seeds

1 tablespoon finely chopped fresh chives

1 pound green asparagus spears (36 pencil-thin, 24 crayon-thick, or 12 very thick)

12 pieces thinly sliced pancetta (3 ounces)

2 tablespoons olive oil

Freshly ground black pepper

MAKES 4 SERVINGS

Place the salt block over low heat on a gas grill grate, close the lid, and warm for 10 minutes (see Read Before Heating!, page 25). Turn the heat to medium and heat for 10 more minutes. Its surface should be about 350°F (see Getting It Hot, page 24).

While the salt block is heating, mix the marmalade, mustard oil, orange juice, olives, mustard seeds, and chives in a small bowl suitable for dipping; set aside.

Cut or snap the tough ends off the asparagus and wrap the asparagus in a piece of pancetta. If using thin asparagus, wrap in bundles of three; if using medium-thick, wrap in pairs; and if using thick mommas, wrap individually. Brush the wrapped asparagus with the olive oil and season with pepper.

Put the asparagus bundles on the hot salt block, close the lid, and grill until the pancetta has rendered about one-quarter of its fat and is beginning to crisp on the bottom, about 4 minutes. The asparagus will turn brighter green. Turn the bundles over, close the lid, and grill until the pancetta is cooked on the other side, about 3 more minutes. Serve with the dipping sauce.

Salt-Seared Sweet Potato Pancakes with Hot Pepper Honey

Grab the words sweet, salt, crunch, fatty, starchy, healthy, and vermilion from a bag. Throw them into the air like a handful of polychrome confetti and watch them glint and tumble through motes of afternoon sunlight. Don't try to make sense of it. Your salt block will take care of that for you. So grab another handful and wad it up into a patty and fry it into a golden fritter. Dip in spicy honey and munch with a minty cool tamarind margarita, or serve it with venison, squab, or ceviche.

1 (10-inch) square salt block

¼ cup honey

1 tablespoon mild hot pepper sauce, like crystal or Frank's RedHot

1 pound orange-fleshed sweet potatoes

2 eggs, lightly beaten

2 tablespoons unbleached all-purpose flour

½ teaspoon medium-fine sea salt, such as fleur de sel

½ teaspoon freshly ground black pepper

1 garlic clove, minced

½ inch fresh ginger, peeled and finely grated

Vegetable oil, to coat the block

MAKES 4 SERVINGS

Place the salt block over low heat on a stovetop burner for 10 minutes (see Read Before Heating!, page 25). Turn the heat to medium and heat for 10 more minutes. Raise the heat to medium-high and heat the block to about 400°F, 5 more minutes (see Getting It Hot, page 24).

Mix the honey and hot sauce in a small bowl until combined; set aside.

Meanwhile grate the sweet potatoes coarsely (you need about 2 cups) and rinse well in a large bowl of cold water. Drain and wring dry in a clean kitchen towel. Put the sweet potatoes back in the bowl and add the eggs, flour, salt, pepper, garlic, and ginger.

When the block is hot, coat the surface with a thin film of oil. Fry heaping soupspoonfuls of the potato batter, flattening the mounds so that they form pancakes about 3 inches diameter. You should get 8 pancakes. Brown well, 4 to 5 minutes per side.

Transfer to a platter and serve with the hot pepper honey.

Salt-Roasted Poultry Gizzards Seasoned with Pastrami Pepper

Sometimes inspiration comes from chaste memory, sometimes from an appetite from out of the shadows of your heart, and sometimes from the synapses of your mind, twisted and casting sparks like power lines downed in a rainstorm. I was in the mood for the savory warm *salade de gésiers de canard* served from a Marseille train station café, but fried up salt block–style. What I got was peppery, salty, aromatic little tidbits fit to serve on toast with unsalted butter, schmaltz, or sharp cheddar. Spicy moist chewy Jewish jerky. What the heck? Inspiration owes you nothing. This is a good thing.

1 large salt block, at least 9 inches square and 1½ inches, tempered (see page 30)

1 tablespoon freshly ground coriander seeds

1 tablespoon freshly ground black peppercorns

1 tablespoon freshly ground white peppercorns

1 teaspoon ground allspice

8 garlic cloves, minced

¼ cup sweet paprika

2 tablespoons dark brown sugar

2 tablespoons molasses

2 pounds chicken, turkey, and/or duck gizzards

1 tablespoon vegetable oil

MAKES 4 SERVINGS

Place the coriander seeds, both peppercorns, allspice, and garlic in a spice grinder or mortar and pestle and grind into a paste. Scrape into a medium bowl and stir in the paprika, brown sugar, and molasses.

Each gizzard will have 2 to 3 lobes of red muscle attached by tough white membrane. Cut away the thick pieces of white membrane and slice the lobes thinly. Discard the membrane. You will get about 1 pound servable meat. Toss the sliced gizzards in the spice mixture and refrigerate for 1 to 2 hours.

Meanwhile, put the tempered salt block on a heavy baking sheet and place on the middle rack of the oven. Turn the oven to 350°F, and heat the block for 1 hour (see Read Before Heating!, page 25).

When the block is hot, coat the spiced gizzards with the oil and spread onto the hot block. Roast until tender, about 40 minutes, scraping and turning the meat about halfway through. Serve as desired (see headnote).

Salt-Baked Walnut Brioche Scones

The ascendancy of the coffee shop in American culture has brought advancements: We get to mooch other people's newspapers, and the Wi-Fi is free. But these unmitigated gains come at a price: bad scones. Where once the scone was a downy bed across which lounged an odalisque of butter or clotted cream, nude but for a necklace of golden honey or a garnet jewel of fruit jam, now we have an overstuffed thrift store sofa hogged by addicts of sugar and spice. There is no easy path back to the true scone, so here's a fresh start. Cakier than brioche, eggier than a scone, sweetly salted, this is a scone that will get you brewing your coffee at home again.

1 large salt block, at least 9 inches square and 1½ inches thick, or at least 3 smaller salt blocks, tempered (see page 30)

1½ cups unbleached all-purpose flour

½ cup sugar

1½ teaspoons baking powder

Pinch of fine Himalayan salt

6 tablespoons softened unsalted butter, cut into 12 pieces

6 extra-large egg yolks

¼ cup heavy cream

1 cup chopped walnuts

MAKES 8 SCONES

Place the tempered salt block(s) on a heavy baking sheet and place on the middle rack of the oven. Turn the oven to 350°F, and heat the block for 1 hour (see Read Before Heating!, page 25).

In the work bowl of a food processor equipped with a steel blade, combine the flour, sugar, baking powder, and salt. Process in short pulses to combine. Add the butter and process in 2 to 3 pulses until it is dispersed evenly. Add the egg yolks and cream and process until the mixture becomes a cohesive dough, about 40 seconds. Add the walnuts and process in pulses until combined, but not so much that the walnuts become finely ground.

Turn the dough out onto a clean work surface and pat into a 9-inch circle about ¾ inch thick. Cut into 8 wedges. Arrange the cut scones on the hot salt block and bake until puffed and browned, about 18 minutes.

Remove from the salt block with a spatula and let cool on a rack for 5 minutes before serving.

Salt-Seared Pineapple Steaks with Curried Agave Drizzle

Pineapple is certainly one of the great flavors, a tropical jungle of tangy deliciousness. But like any jungle with its macaws and howler monkeys, pineapple can be pretty overwhelming with its sugary stridency and piercing acidity. A salt block can fix this. Thick steaks of pineapple seared on a salt block almost cease to register as a fruit at all, much less an overly sweet one. The texture is all meaty tenderness, a caramelized complexity calms us, and the sugars and acids are stilled by the silent thunderclap of salt, turning the sweltering bush into a rain forest paradise. This dish makes a perfect side for savory pork or seafood dishes, or featured as a dessert with a dollop of crème fraîche or a drizzle of melted chocolate.

1 (9- to 10-inch) square salt block

⅓ cup agave syrup

Finely grated zest and juice of
½ orange

2 tablespoons dark rum

1 teaspoon curry powder

3 tablespoons unsalted butter, cut into pieces

1 small pineapple (about 2 pounds)

MAKES 4 SERVINGS

Place the salt block over low heat on a gas grill or stovetop burner for 10 minutes (see Read Before Heating!, page 25). Turn the heat to medium and heat for 10 more minutes. Raise the heat to medium-high and heat the block to about 400°F, 5 more minutes (see Getting It Hot, page 24).

Put the agave, orange zest and juice, rum, and curry powder in a small saucepan. Bring to a boil over high heat, then lower the heat to medium-high and cook until reduced to about ⅓ cup. Remove from the heat and whisk in the butter. Set aside.

Cut off the spiky top of the pineapple and ½ inch from the base. Stand upright and cut downward around the fruit to remove the peel and eyes. Cut into 1-inch-thick rounds.

Put the pineapple steaks on the hot block (you will have to cook in batches) and cook until bright yellow, 2 to 3 minutes per side. Brush with some of the glaze and cook until browned, about 2 minutes more per side. Transfer to a platter and brush with more glaze. Repeat with the remaining slices. Serve warm.

Cinnamon Salt Plantains with Lemon-Espresso Syrup

The Mayan woman who cooked the best fried plantains I've ever eaten looked shocked when I sprinkled a few crystals of fresh Pacific sea salt over them, altering the recipe that had been in her family since time out of mind. We were sitting in the orange-purple morning, watching the herons yo-yo over the mangrove-forested perimeter of the salt farm where I had just scooped salt, dripping with silken minerals from the still waters. Lacking any of Guatemala's twenty-one Mayan languages and uncertain of our mutual Spanish, I simply proffered her my fork, at the end of which steamed a succulent slice of fried plantain bejeweled with the fresh salt from her front yard. Whether it was the act of being fed from a white man's fork or the taste of her own plantain, salted, I'll never know, but her eyes shone with a black warmth like coffee in a simmering steel pot. Just because it hasn't been done before doesn't mean it isn't the natural thing to do. Plantains fried on a salt block are even more delicious.

1 (8- to 10-inch) square salt or (9-inch) round block

½ cup sugar

1 tablespoon ground Vietnamese cinnamon

4 ripe black plantains (see Note), peeled, cut at a 45-degree angle into ¾-inch-thick ovals

¾ cup brewed espresso

Pinch of ground cloves

¼ cup lemon marmalade

2 tablespoons honey

1 tablespoon mild vegetable oil

MAKES 4 SERVINGS

Place the salt block over low heat on a gas grill or stovetop burner for 10 minutes (see Read Before Heating!, page 25). Turn the heat to medium and heat for 10 more minutes. Raise the heat to medium-high and heat the block to about 400°F, 5 more minutes (see Getting It Hot, page 24).

While the block is heating, mix the sugar and cinnamon on a plate. Coat the plantain slices in the cinnamon sugar and set aside.

Make the glaze by combining the espresso, cloves, marmalade, and honey in a small bowl; set aside.

When the block is hot, drizzle the plantain slices with the oil, and brown on both sides on the hot salt block, about 1 minute, turning them with a sharp metal spatula halfway through. As you turn them, make sure to scrape up any crisp bits that may be clinging to the block.

Serve with the espresso syrup spooned over the top or on the side for dipping.

NOTE: To ripen green plantains to black, put in a closed paper bag for 2 to 3 days.

Salt Crust Cardamom Naan

Naan is the generic term for the many types of flatbreads eaten across South Asia. It's distinguished from other breads largely by the technique of cooking it, slapping the dough against the clay walls of an oven called a tandoor. This tandoori bread has emerged as a global favorite. The only way to improve on such success is to innovate from the inside, so to speak. Instead of mere hot clay, slap your naan dough against a salt block mined from the dark womb of Asia's famous Mughal-era salt mines. Delicate crispiness on the edges and delectable elasticity everywhere else, with the satisfying savoriness of salt coming from the soul of the bread: your innovative yet authentic salt block tandoor.

1 large salt block, at least 9 inches square and 1½ inches thick, tempered (see page 30)

1 teaspoon active dry yeast

¾ cup warm water (about 110°F)

½ cup plain yogurt

1½ teaspoons ground cardamom

1½ cups bread flour

1 tablespoon canola oil, plus more for coating the breads

2 teaspoons sugar

Finely ground kala namak (Indian black salt)

1 cup whole wheat flour, or as needed

2 teaspoons unsalted butter, softened

MAKES 8 SERVINGS

Mix the yeast and ¼ cup of the warm water in a large bowl until the yeast has dissolved.

Mix the yogurt, 1 teaspoon of the cardamom, and the remaining ½ cup warm water in a medium bowl and stir into the yeast mixture until everything is blended. Add the bread flour and stir vigorously for 2 minutes. Cover loosely with plastic wrap and set aside at room temperature until bubbly, about 30 minutes.

Stir in the 1 tablespoon oil, the sugar, a pinch of salt, and enough of the whole wheat flour to make a kneadable dough. Knead on a clean work surface using additional bread flour to keep the dough from sticking until the dough is smooth and elastic.

Coat a large bowl lightly with oil. Turn the dough in the oiled bowl to coat with oil; cover with plastic wrap and let rise at room temperature until doubled in bulk, about 1 hour.

Meanwhile, put the tempered salt block on a heavy baking sheet and place on the bottom rack of the oven. Turn the oven to 350°F, and heat the block for 15 minutes. Turn the oven up to 450°F and heat for another 15 minutes. Turn the oven up to 550°F and heat for 15 to 20 more minutes.

Divide the dough into quarters; roll each into a ball and flatten into a ½-inch-thick disk. Cover with a lint-free kitchen towel and let rest for 5 minutes.

Lightly flour a clean work surface with bread flour and roll each disk of dough into a long oval (about 9 inches long and about ¼ inch thick). Coat each oval with canola oil and stack on a plate.

Put one of the breads on the hot salt block and bake until browned and puffed, about 4 minutes. Remove using tongs and repeat with the remaining three breads. As soon as each bread comes out of the oven, brush with the butter and sprinkle with a little of the remaining ½ teaspoon ground cardamom and a pinch of salt.

BLACK SALT

Try your naan with a little *kala namak*. This savory, umami-fueled condiment also known as black salt is a distinctive element in South Asian cooking. It is made by melting salts such as Himalayan rock salt in pots with a variety of botanicals. *Kala namak* has a head-spinning eggy sulfuric taste that is not subtle, but for that very reason, it is a thrill to use. A pinch sprinkled on naan lends an irreducible authenticity and lets you know you're eating something that is not just yummy and a touch exotic but also big and bold and unique as South Asia itself.

Salt-Griddled Blini with Sour Cream and Salt-Cured Candied Strawberries

Secret agents named Natasha have a penchant for blinis topped with the nutty-metallic plumpness of osetra caviar, while discus throwers named Pishchalnikova can't do without blinis with blueberry treacle. Both hale from Old World kitchens, with their thick-walled love for rich saltiness and muscular sweetness. Like a knitted wool shirt, they seem unnecessarily comforting, unbefitting the lucent rooms of modern life. But savory-sweet strawberries tucked into voluptuous sour cream on a fluffy salt-crisped buckwheat pancake bring blini within striking distance of the here and now.

1 (10-inch) square salt block

¼ cup buckwheat flour

¼ cup whole wheat flour

½ cup unbleached all-purpose flour

1 teaspoon baking powder

½ teaspoon baking soda

1 teaspoon sugar

¼ teaspoon fine sea salt, such as fleur de sel

1 egg, separated

1 cup buttermilk

2 tablespoons unsalted butter, melted

Vegetable oil, for coating the salt block

½ cup sour cream

12 fresh or Salt-Cured Candied Strawberries (page 70)

MAKE 4 SERVINGS

Place the salt block over low heat on a stovetop burner for 10 minutes (see Read Before Heating!, page 25). Turn the heat to medium and heat for 10 more minutes. Raise the heat to medium-high and heat the block to about 400°F, 5 more minutes (see Getting It Hot, page 24).

As soon as the block is hot, mix the buckwheat, whole wheat, and all-purpose flours, baking powder, baking soda, sugar, and salt in a large bowl. Add the egg yolk and buttermilk and mix just enough so that everything is moistened. Stir in the melted butter.

In a clean separate bowl, beat the egg white using a large whisk until it forms soft peaks (just holds a shape). Do not overbeat. Fold into the batter.

Coat the surface of the hot block with a thin film of oil. Spoon batter onto the hot block to form small pancakes, about 2 inches across each, leaving about 1 inch between them. Cook until crisp and brown on the bottom and set up at the sides, about 2 minutes. Flip with a spatula and cook on the other side until puffed and browned on the bottom. Transfer to a plate with a spatula and keep warm. Cook the remaining batter and serve the blini with dollops of sour cream and strawberries.

Salt-Baked Rustic Apple-Onion Tart with Blue Cheese

The savory rustic tart is one of the biggest contributors to the good name of rustic food. The non-rustic version can't beat it. No level of refinement, no phyllo dough crust, no olives and anchovies and herbs, not even calling it a pissaladière can tip the scales. Cooking it on a salt block elevates the tart without diminishing its essential rusticity. The salt block baking creates a crust as good as a wood-fired Neapolitan pizza, but with a little salt-shocked zing to help carry the caramelized apples and onions. Rustic, yes, but also perfect.

1 large salt block, at least 9 inches square and 1½ inches thick, tempered (see page 30)

3 large yellow onions, quartered and sliced

1 large tart apple, peeled, cored, and cut into thin wedges

2 tablespoons olive oil

Sel gris and freshly ground black pepper

1½ cups unbleached all-purpose flour

4 ounces (1 stick) unsalted butter, cut into small pieces

¼ cup cold milk

Handful of cornmeal

1 ounce blue cheese, crumbled

MAKES 8 SERVINGS

Place the tempered salt block on the bottom rack of the oven (see Read Before Heating!, page 25). Turn the oven to 350°F, and heat the block for 20 minutes. Turn the oven to 400°F and heat for another 25 minutes.

Toss the onions, apple, and oil on a large rimmed baking sheet. Season with salt and pepper to taste, and bake for 30 minutes, or until lightly browned and soft.

Meanwhile, make the pastry by combining the flour, butter, and a pinch of black pepper in the work bowl of a food processor. Process in pulses until the butter is uniformly cut into the flour; add the milk and keep processing until the mixture is moist and climbs the side of the bowl. Remove the dough from the processor and pat together into a flat disk. Roll on a lightly floured board into a rough disk about 14 inches across and ¼ inch thick.

Sprinkle a rimless baking sheet or a pizza peel with cornmeal. Place the pastry disk on the cornmeal-covered surface. Mound the apple and onions in the center of the pastry and flatten into a 9½-inch circle. Fold the edges of the dough over the filling; some of the filling in the middle will remain exposed. Slip the tart from the pan onto the hot salt block. Bake for 25 to 35 minutes, until browned and crisp. Sprinkle the top with the blue cheese and let cool for at least 15 minutes before cutting into wedges and serving.

Salt Block Baked Pretzel Rolls with Mustard Butter

Baked on a salt block, pretzels gain a salty crispy crust that would be the envy of any New York City snack cart vendor. Unknot your pretzel, roll it into a roll, and the improvement is only more striking. These pretzel rolls have all the salt-spiked deliciousness of the best pretzel, but with an even better yeasty, chewy, tender, doughy inside. A sprinkle of smoked salt and a smear of mustard butter take these from sidewalk snack to dining room delicacy.

3 (8-inch) square salt blocks, at least 1½ inches thick, tempered (see page 30)

1 cup warm water (110°F to 115°F)

2 teaspoons active dry yeast

1 teaspoon sugar

¼ cup extra-virgin olive oil

2¾ cups bread flour, plus more as needed

2 teaspoons fleur de sel

2 tablespoons unsalted butter, softened

2 teaspoons whole-grain mustard

3 tablespoons baking soda

¼ cup cornmeal

1 to 2 tablespoons coarse smoked salt

MAKES 12 ROLLS

Combine the water, yeast, and sugar in a large bowl, stirring until mixed. Let sit until foamy, about 5 minutes. Stir in 3 tablespoons of the olive oil, the flour, and fleur de sel and stir into a kneadable dough.

Turn onto a floured work surface and knead until the dough is smooth and elastic, about 5 minutes. Add more bread flour as needed to keep the dough from sticking to your hands or the work surface. However, try to add as little flour as possible.

Coat a large bowl with the remaining 1 tablespoon oil and add the dough, turning to coat it with the oil. Cover and let rise in a warm spot until doubled in bulk, about 1 hour, or overnight in the refrigerator.

Meanwhile, line the bottom rack of the oven with the tempered salt blocks (see Read Before Heating!, page 25). Turn the oven to 350°F, and heat the block for 20 minutes. Turn the oven to 425°F and heat for another 25 minutes.

In a small bowl, mash the softened butter and mustard with a fork until thoroughly combined. Transfer to a ramekin.

Bring 4 cups water to a boil in a large deep skillet. Add the baking soda and stir to dissolve, adjusting the heat so that the water just simmers. Sprinkle a baking sheet with the cornmeal.

Cut the dough into 12 pieces. Roll a piece into a ball, then stretch the top of the ball over itself, making a sort of seashell shape, and then squeeze the edges together to a point so you have a shiny ball. Push down each roll to create flatter rolls roughly the shape of bagels without holes. Set the rolls, one at a time, in the simmering water and simmer until they puff, about 20 seconds per side. Lift them with a slotted spatula or spoon, allowing the excess water to drip back into the skillet before putting them on the cornmeal-coated baking sheet. Sprinkle the tops of the rolls with the smoked salt, and put the rolls on the salt blocks. Bake until golden brown, 12 to 15 minutes. Transfer to a cooling rack and let cool for at least 10 minutes before serving with the mustard butter.

Salt-Baked Chocolate Chip–Oatmeal Whoppers

"You're traveling through another dimension, a dimension not only of sight and sound but of mind. A journey into a wondrous land whose boundaries are that of imagination." Salt is the one substance that can magically transport a flavor from one place to another, from the present into the beyond. Chocolate chip cookies are a case in point. With every layer, the food travels through another dimension. A pinch of salt dust dissolved in the batter, a few architectural crystals flung on top, and a whole time-space continuum of just-perceptible salt along the bottom. Rod Serling couldn't have said it better.

1 (8 by 12 by 2-inch) salt block, or 3 (4 by 8 by 2-inch) salt blocks, tempered (see page 30)

1 cup unbleached all-purpose flour

1 cup old-fashioned or quick-cooking rolled oats (not instant)

½ teaspoon baking soda

½ teaspoon ground cinnamon

Pinch of fine Himalayan salt

4 ounces (1 stick) unsalted butter, cut into chunks and softened

¾ cup light brown sugar

1 large or extra-large egg

1 teaspoon vanilla extract

1 cup semisweet chocolate chips

Pinch of dry flaked salt, such as Halen Môn, Bali Kechil, or Maldon

MAKES 10 LARGE COOKIES

Place the tempered salt block(s) on a heavy baking sheet and place on the middle rack of the oven (see Read Before Heating!, page 25). Turn the oven to 350°F, and heat the block(s) for 1 hour.

Mix the flour, oats, baking soda, cinnamon, and Himalayan salt in a medium bowl.

Mix the butter and sugar in a large bowl with a wooden spoon or with an electric mixer using the paddle attachment until creamy. Mix in the egg and vanilla. Mix in the dry ingredients just until a cohesive dough forms. Stir in the chocolate chips.

Line a baking sheet or large flat plate with aluminum foil. Divide the dough into 10 equal portions (about ⅓ cup each). Wet your hands with cold water and form each piece of dough into a ball. Arrange on the foil. Flatten into ½-inch-thick disks and sprinkle with the flaked salt.

With wet hands, lift the cookies off the foil and arrange on the hot salt block(s), 1 to 1½ inches apart. Bake until set, browned on the bottom and dry on the top, but still soft, about 10 minutes. Transfer with a spatula to a cooling rack and let cool for at least 10 minutes before devouring.

CHAPTER 5

CHILLING ON SALT BLOCKS

Salt-Frozen Mocha–Panna Cotta Gelato

Salt-Frozen Parmesan Ice Cream with
Tomato Marmalade and Basil Gremolata

Salted Bitters Ice Cream

Salt-Cured Strawberry Ice Cream

Chocolate-Covered Salt-Sopped Cherries

Salted Peanut Brittle

Fleur de Salt Block Caramels

Gold-Crusted Salty Chocolate Curls

Oblique rays of sun plunge into polar ice and seem to disappear forever, with only a blue-silver glow emerging, like an optical echo from the past. There is something captivating about ice and the frozen realm it inhabits, its permanence and its transience. Woolly mammoth jerky found freeze-dried in glaciers contrasts with the evanescence of ice cream. Freezing a half-billion-year-old salt block creates a halide ice that is mind-bendingly ancient.

The first time I laid my hands on my new, 2-inch-thick, 10-inch square salt block that I had had specially made for myself, I realized I didn't know quite what to do with it. It wasn't giving me any clues. I still have it, and still it has very little to say for itself. It is freaking massive, weighs a solid 16 pounds, and, I kid you not, there is a palpable air of smugness about it. That's what initially attracted me to it: its supremely confident bulk. For some reason I wanted to freeze it. So I tossed out some forgotten tubs of veal stock at the back of the freezer and put the block in for the night.

Drinking a Sazerac while pacing the kitchen at midnight, it came to me. I made up a custard, poured in a few teaspoons of aromatic bitters, stuck it in the fridge, and went to bed. For breakfast I drizzled the chilled custard over the frozen salt block, lifting and folding it with a spatula as it set, to make an aromatic bitters soft-serve ice cream (see page 176). Robust, almost ribald in flavor, it was so clearly the imagining of a pacing man up late at night drinking Sazeracs that it was a bit embarrassing to eat in the beams of morning sun—but the sexy tingle of salted smugness made up for it. There is nothing similar to salt block ice cream.

The colder the salt block, the more radical the reaction between your food and the block. Bathing a salt block in liquid nitrogen and then scrambling some mango puree on top creates this crazy, barely salted tropical stuff with a texture that lies somewhere between whipped cream and cotton candy. On a less extreme note, the freezer cools a salt block to just the right place for making luscious Parmesan ice cream (see page 174), savory strawberry ice cream (see page 179), and mocha–panna cotta gelato (see page 173).

Weirdly, the opposite is true as well. The *less* cold the salt block, the more radical the reaction between your food and the block. Lightly cooling two salt blocks in the refrigerator and compressing fresh cherries between them concentrates their flavors for a crazy salt-candied cherry confabulation that is begging to be dipped in chocolate (see page 181). And of course, salt blocks can even excel at doing nothing much to speak of. Pour dark chocolate over a cool salt block and scrape it up to make chocolate curls (see page 190) salted just this side of not at all.

Contrariness is part of the salt block's nature. This is the essence of what is exciting about chilling on salt blocks. The thermal mass of the block freezes the food, but the salt raises the freezing point of the liquids, thawing it. There is a wonderful tension as the food transitions from liquid to solid, and from solid right back to an aqueous precipice. Like a golden diver stopped midair over aquamarine waters, the mind thrills when boundaries between extreme states are split by something so unsettling as time.

Salt-Frozen Mocha–Panna Cotta Gelato

Walk the streets of San Gimignano at midnight, towers floodlit in greens and turquoises and scarlets, and pause for a moment of excruciating indecision. The gelateria and the café are both closing up, and you have to make a mad dash to either one or the other. Which will it be, gelato or panna cotta? Freeze the dilemma forever in your mind and season it with a cirrus of salt swirled into it.

1 (8- to 10-inch) square or (9-inch) round salt block

1 (¼-ounce) packet unflavored gelatin (about 2 teaspoons)

½ cup brewed espresso, at room temperature or cooler

1 cup half-and-half

1 cup heavy cream

½ cup sugar

3 ounces semisweet chocolate, finely chopped

MAKES 4 SERVINGS

Chill the salt block in the freezer for at least 4 hours, or up to several days.

Sprinkle the gelatin over the espresso in a small bowl.

Mix the half-and-half, cream, and sugar in a medium saucepan. Heat over medium heat, stirring from time to time, just until tiny bubbles form around the edges of the pan, 3 to 4 minutes. Remove from the heat.

Put the chocolate in a medium bowl. Add the hot cream mixture and stir until the chocolate is melted and incorporated. Add the gelatin mixture and stir until the gelatin is completely dissolved. Let cool to room temperature, and refrigerate overnight.

Remove the panna cotta mixture from the refrigerator and mix with a whisk to loosen the mixture. Pour about half of the cold panna cotta mixture onto the frozen block and slough with a sturdy metal spatula until the ice cream sets up. Transfer to a 1-quart container, seal, and freeze. Freeze the remaining mixture on the salt block, transfer to the container, and freeze until ready to serve, up to 24 hours.

Salt-Frozen Parmesan Ice Cream with Tomato Marmalade and Basil Gremolata

Forget everything you ever knew. Ice cream isn't sweet and tomatoes aren't tangy. Basil is a dessert topping and Parmesan is a silken river frozen over a waterless sea.

1 (8- to 10-inch) square or (9-inch) round salt block

Ice Cream

5 cups heavy cream

8 ounces Parmigiano-Reggiano, freshly grated

Marmalade

1 pound plum tomatoes, peeled and coarsely chopped

⅓ cup sugar

1½ tablespoons sherry vinegar

1 tablespoon extra-virgin olive oil (the best you can afford)

Gremolata

12 fresh basil leaves, finely chopped

¼ garlic clove, minced

½ cup chopped toasted hazelnuts

1 tablespoon finely grated lemon zest

To Finish

2 tablespoons olive oil (the best you can afford)

MAKES 6 SERVINGS

Chill the salt block in the freezer for 6 hours before you want to finish the ice cream.

To make the ice cream, bring the cream to a simmer in a large saucepan. Add the cheese slowly, stirring all the time, and continue to simmer and stir over low heat until the cheese has melted and the mixture is smooth, about 5 minutes. Pass through a strainer to remove any lumps, and let cool to room temperature. Put in a closed container and chill thoroughly in the refrigerator for several hours or overnight.

An hour before you want to finish the ice cream, put the container of ice cream mixture in the freezer.

To make the marmalade, cook the tomatoes, sugar, and vinegar in a medium saucepan, stirring frequently until lightly thickened, about 15 minutes. Stir in the olive oil and let cool to room temperature.

To make the gremolata, mix the basil, garlic, hazelnuts, and lemon zest together in a small bowl.

To finish the ice cream, put the frozen salt block on a rimmed baking sheet to catch any drips. Spoon half of the chilled ice cream mixture onto the frozen salt block, using a pastry scraper or the side of a spatula to control its flow. Scrape and fold the ice cream across the surface of the salt until it sets up. Scrape into a chilled bowl put in the freezer while repeating the process with the remaining half of the ice cream mixture.

To serve, scoop the ice cream into chilled bowls. Drizzle each serving with the olive oil, and top each with a spoonful of marmalade and a sprinkling of gremolata.

Salted Bitters Ice Cream

Salty, savory, sour, and sweet are the rulers of snacks, meals, dressing, and desserts. Bitters, the sole B flavor, sits alone in sepia shadows, the villain wringing its fingers, scheming to vanquish its foes and transcend its ignominy. But offer poor bitters an olive branch, or less figuratively, a salt block, and the villain reveals himself as a noble figure. His first act of grace is to make ice cream fit for a king. Try this recipe with any type of cocktail bitters: aromatic, orange, cherry bark, cardamom, or licorice, to name a few.

1 (8- to 10-inch) square or (9-inch) round salt block

3 cups half-and-half

⅔ cup sugar

4 extra-large egg yolks

1 to 2 tablespoons cocktail bitters of your choice

¼ teaspoon vanilla extract

MAKES 4 SERVINGS

Chill the salt block in the freezer for at least 4 hours, or up to several days.

Mix the half-and-half and sugar in a medium saucepan. Heat over medium heat, stirring from time to time, just until tiny bubbles form around the edges of the pan, 3 to 4 minutes. Remove from the heat. Slowly mix ¼ cup of the hot half-and-half into the egg yolks in a small bowl. Add another ¼ cup of the half-and-half, and then stir that mixture back into the saucepan. Cook over medium-low heat, stirring constantly, until slightly thickened (180°F). Remove from the heat and let cool for 10 minutes, or until the mixture is at room temperature. Stir in the bitters and vanilla. Put in a closed container and chill thoroughly in the refrigerator for several hours or overnight.

Pour about half of the cold custard onto the frozen salt block and slough with a sturdy rubber spatula until the ice cream sets up. Transfer to a 1-quart container, seal, and put in the freezer. Freeze the remaining custard mixture on the salt block, transfer to the container, and freeze until ready to serve, up to 24 hours.

Salt-Cured Strawberry Ice Cream

Ice cream is the roller coaster of foods. I make this claim on the basis that it is the food for which I scream, you scream, we all scream. And of all the flavors, perhaps none makes us scream more than the time-honored classic, strawberry. But while the makers of roller coasters clearly enjoy making their rides ever more scream-worthy, strawberry ice cream has remained pretty much a simple arc of sweet, strawberry, and . . . sweet. Salt-curing the strawberries and then freezing the ice cream on salt lifts this familiar flavor up, up, up into the air and then releases it for a crazed rush of sweet, savory, sweet, strawberry, savory, sweet, creamy, salt, strawberry that a quiet voice could never express.

1 (9- to 10-inch) square salt block, at least 2 inches thick

1 vanilla bean, split lengthwise

2 cups half-and-half

½ cup sugar

4 extra-large egg yolks

12 Salt-Cured Candied Strawberries (page 70)

½ teaspoon vanilla extract

MAKES 4 SERVINGS

Chill the salt block in the freezer for at least 4 hours, or up to several days.

Put the split vanilla bean in a medium saucepan. Add the half-and-half and sugar. Heat over medium heat, stirring from time to time, just until tiny bubbles form around the edges of the pan, 3 to 4 minutes. Remove from the heat.

Slowly mix ¼ cup of the hot half-and-half into the egg yolks in a small bowl. Add another ¼ cup of the half-and-half, and then stir that mixture back into the saucepan. Cook over medium-low heat, stirring constantly, until slightly thickened (180°F). Remove from the heat and let cool for 10 minutes, or until the mixture is at room temperature. Remove the vanilla bean.

Remove the greens from the strawberries and mash into a coarse puree with the back of a large fork. Stir into the ice cream, along with the vanilla. Cover and refrigerate until thoroughly chilled, several hours or overnight.

Pour about half of the cold custard onto the frozen block and slough with a sturdy rubber spatula until the ice cream sets up. Transfer to a 1-quart container, seal, and freeze. Freeze the remaining custard mixture on the salt block, transfer to the container, and freeze until ready to serve, up to 24 hours.

Chocolate-Covered Salt-Sopped Cherries

The sun is a 50-trillion-kiloton ball of fusion, and so it doesn't care for winter. When it finally gets out in the spring, it is looking for something to do with all its pent-up energy. After messing around with daffodils and whatnot, it dedicates itself to the more serious work of packing all its high-explosive energy into cherries. Pop a cherry in your mouth and pow! But by then the sun has already moved on to other things, like oak trees and sunbathers. So pressing those cherries under a salt block, compacting the flavors to the bursting point, is just continuing the sun's good work planting a land mine of flavor in a fruit orchard.

2 (4 by 8 by 2-inch) salt blocks

12 large sweet cherries, pitted

¼ cup sugar

6 ounces semisweet chocolate, finely chopped

MAKES 12 CANDIES

Chill the salt blocks in the refrigerator for at least 2 hours, or up to several days.

Remove the blocks from the refrigerator and put one of them on a baking sheet that will catch any drips from the cherries.

Space the cherries evenly in a single layer on the block. Carefully place the other block squarely on top so that it balances evenly on all of the cherries. Set aside until the cherries are lightly compressed, 3 to 6 hours, depending on ripeness. As the fruit cures, it will lose about 50 percent of its water, concentrating the cherry flavor.

Remove the cherries from the blocks, wipe the blocks clean, and return to the refrigerator. Remove any lingering moisture from the cherries with paper towels, and then toss in a bowl with the sugar. Set aside for 1 hour.

Put half of the chocolate in the top of a double boiler or in a microwave-safe bowl. If using the double boiler, put over gently simmering water and stir until melted. If using the microwave, cover the bowl and microwave at full power for 1½ minutes. Stir until smooth. Remove from the heat, and stir the remaining half of the chocolate into the melted chocolate until the mixture is completely melted and smooth.

Remove the salt blocks from the refrigerator. Lift the cherries from the sugar and pat dry. Dip the cherries, one at a time, in the chocolate and remove with a fork, allowing excess chocolate to drip back into the bowl. Put the dipped cherry on the chilled salt block; repeat with the remaining cherries and chocolate. Set aside until the chocolate is completely hard. Serve within 24 hours.

Salted Peanut Brittle

Nuts are naturally high in both fat and protein. This is a boringly scientific observation that does nothing to explain why we love nuts, but it does help us to figure out how to make the most of them. The protein in nuts is what gives them their flavor. The fat gives them their irresistibly toothsome crunch. Suspending nuts in a galaxy of caramelized sugar boosts the flavor of the proteins, but knocks things out of kilter because the fat is left with nothing to do with itself. Salt restores balance to the flavors and then rockets everything into the stratosphere. Put more simply: Peanut brittle tastes better with salt. Here the salt block provides a cool surface for setting up the brittle, but it is unable to offer salt of its own due to the absence of moisture in the brittle, so finely ground Himalayan salt is added in sympathy. Try this recipe with other finely ground nuts, such as pine nuts, walnuts, or almonds. Or take a walk on the wild side and make a salt brittle with some coarse Himalayan rock salt or a smashed up salt block!

1 (10 by 10 or 8 by 12-inch) salt block

1 tablespoon unsalted butter, plus more for coating the block and spatula

1 cup sugar

2 tablespoons agave syrup

1 cup unsalted roasted peanuts

Pinch of baking soda

1 tablespoon coarse Himalayan pink salt

MAKES ABOUT ¾ POUND

Grease the salt block with a thin film of butter. Chill the buttered block in the refrigerator for at least 1 hour, or up to several days.

Put the sugar in a large nonstick skillet and cook over medium-high heat, stirring occasionally with a wooden spoon, until the sugar begins to melt and lump up, about 4 minutes. Add the agave syrup. The mixture will start to foam. Stir constantly. The liquid sugar will steadily become thinner and deep amber, and the lumps will start to melt. Turn the heat off when almost all the lumps are gone and the sugar is a golden color. (Sugar caramelizes at 320°F; nonstick surfaces don't break down until 500°F.)

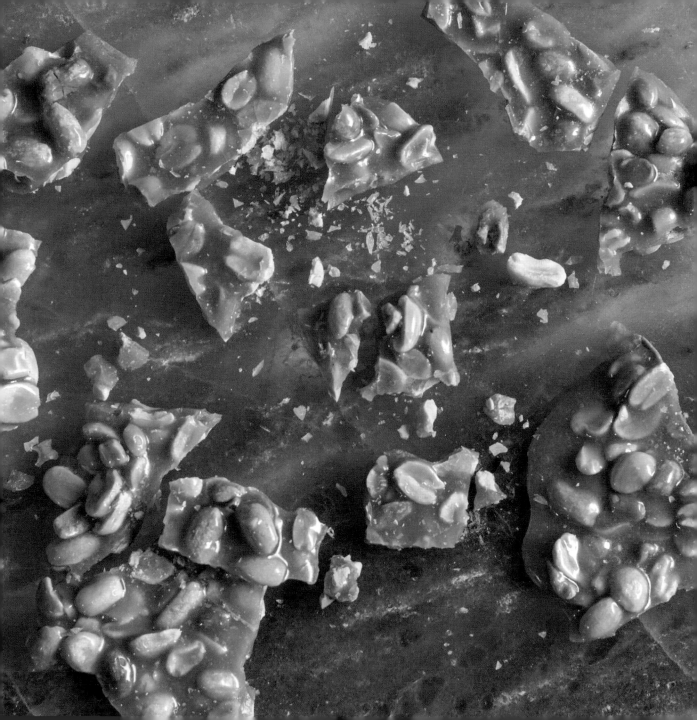

Immediately stir in the peanuts, the 1 tablespoon butter, and the baking soda. The liquid will become very foamy for a second. Stir until the foam is no longer streaky, about 10 seconds, and then immediately pour onto the chilled salt block, scraping as much of the melted sugar from the pan as possible with your wooden spoon.

Sprinkle the salt over the top of the sugar and count to twenty-four. The edges of the sugar pool should be firm. Grease a spatula with some butter and slide your spatula under the sugar to loosen it from the block all of the way around, and then flip it over.

Working quickly, stretch the sheet of sugar as much as you can before it become too brittle to move. The easiest way is to gingerly push it with your hands into a larger thinner sheet about the size and shape of the block. If some parts are thinner than others, don't worry. If your hands are very sensitive to heat, you can wear latex gloves, but it's harder to work the sugar that way, so I advise you to suck it up and use your hands. It won't be that hot. When the brittle is too brittle to move, stop pushing and let it cool.

Break into shards and serve. Store in a closed container at room temperature for up to 1 week.

Fleur de Salt Block Caramels

Caramel lovers fight over who invented the salted caramel, the French or the Americans. It was the French who perfected salted caramels by using precious fleur de sel as the salt. The mineral glitter of fleur de sel elevated caramel (which is incredibly easy to make) from ho-hum candy to globally fêted confection. Score one for France. My motivation for making caramel on a salt block was not so much that I wanted to taste a better caramel as that, as an American, I wanted to taste victory. Referees wanted.

1 (8-inch) square salt block

Nonstick cooking spray

1 cup heavy cream

5 tablespoons unsalted butter, cut into pieces

1½ cups sugar

¼ cup agave syrup

MAKES 64 CARAMELS

Tear off an 18-inch square piece of heavy-duty aluminum foil. Put it on a baking sheet and put the salt block in the center of the foil. Fold the foil up the sides of the block, creasing the corners to make them square as you would when fitting a flat sheet to a mattress. Fold the edge of the foil down all the way around, forming a 2-inch-high foil wall above the surface of the block going all the way around the perimeter. The salt block will now be sitting snugly in a foil "pan." Spray the top of the block and the interior of the foil wall with nonstick cooking spray. Refrigerate the entire setup for at least 2 hours.

When the block is thoroughly chilled, bring the cream and butter to a simmer in a small saucepan; remove from the heat and set aside.

Boil the sugar, agave syrup, and ¼ cup water in a medium saucepan, stirring until the sugar dissolves. Boil, gently swirling the pan (do not stir at this point) until the sugar turns a pale golden color, about 8 minutes.

Carefully stir in the cream mixture (the mixture will bubble vigorously) and simmer, stirring often, until the liquid reaches 248°F on a candy thermometer, about 12 minutes. At that point the concentration of sugar will be about 87 percent and a drop of the mixture dribbled into a glass of cold water will form a ball that will be firm enough to lift up but flexible enough to flatten between your fingers.

Remove the foil-encased salt block from the refrigerator. Pour the hot caramel onto the cold block. The caramel should set instantly, but be careful about pouring too close to the edge, to try to keep the liquid caramel from flowing between the block and the foil wall. Let cool until firm throughout, about 2 hours longer.

Remove the foil and cut the caramel into approximately 1-inch square pieces (8 by 8 grid). Wrap each piece in a 4-inch square of waxed paper or cellophane, twisting the ends to close. Store at room temperature for several weeks. If your environment is humid, put the caramels in a tightly closed container.

Gold-Crusted Salty Chocolate Curls

Chocolate contains practically no moisture, so there is no commingling with salt when you bring the two together. (The friction of scraping the curls off the block does add just an infinitesimal integument of salt, but it's so subtle.) But don't let the absence of salacious excitement put you off. You should always have a chilled salt block on hand to practice the not-so-easy art of making salt block chocolate curls. The more often you gussy up desserts, waffles, and morning granola and fruit parfaits with a few chocolate curls, the happier you will be as a human being. And if you're in the mood, add a few flakes of smoked salt and some 24-karat gold leaf for something truly racy. This recipe is fairly advanced; the chocolate has to be spread at just the right thickness across the block, the block has to be the right temperature, and you'll need a reasonably high-performance pair of hands to scrape the block just the right way. Failed curls can always be remelted to try again, or simply used as chocolate shards. Put the pastry chef in you to task and give it a go.

1 (8 by 12-inch or larger) salt block

3 ounces semisweet chocolate, finely chopped

1 tablespoon vegetable shortening

1 (3½-inch square) sheet edible 23-karat gold leaf

2 teaspoons smoked flaked sea salt, such as Halen Môn Gold or Alaska smoked

MAKES ABOUT 2 CUPS

Chill the salt block in the refrigerator for at least 2 hours, or up to several days.

Put the chocolate and shortening in the top of a double boiler or in a microwave-safe bowl. If using the double boiler, put over gently simmering water and stir until melted. Remove from the heat and let sit for 4 minutes. If using the microwave, cover the bowl and microwave at full power for 1½ minutes. Stir until smooth. Let sit for 4 minutes.

Remove the block from the refrigerator and pour the chocolate across the block. Using an icing spatula or a long knife, spread the chocolate across the block in a thin, even sheet. Sprinkle with the salt. Let sit for about 3 minutes. Touch the chocolate with one finger. The chocolate should be firm but just soft enough for your finger to leave a subtle imprint. If it is too soft, you can either wait another 2 minutes or stick it back in the fridge for a minute and then test again.

To make the curls, scrape the chocolate from the cold block in strips, using a sturdy sharp-edged spatula turned upside down. If the chocolate is too soft, it will not curl (chill for another minute). If it is too hard, the chocolate will break into shards (set out at room temperature for a few minutes). And if it is just right, the chocolate will curl up on itself like a scroll.

When the curls are all made, crumble the gold leaf and sprinkle evenly over the chocolate. Freeze them (still on the block) until hard, about 10 minutes. Store frozen for up to 1 month in a zipper-lock plastic bag with the air sucked out. Use to decorate cakes or to gussy up a bowl of chocolate pudding.

CHAPTER 6

DRINKING FROM SALT CUPS

COOL

Islay Scotch and Chocolate

Double-Fisted Tecate and Mezcal

Quick-Cured Oyster with Gin Sangrita

FROZEN

Iced Pepper Vodka Shooter

Basil Salt Daiquiri

Salacious Julep

Amaro Salato

HOT

Warm Sake Shot with Daikon

Xocolatl Xtabentún

Café Calva

The ancient Greeks philosophized that society is made up of two conflicting forces, which they personified in their gods. The Apollonian force represented the order and industry that made society tick, and the Dionysian force represented the irrepressible chaos of our hearts. You can't have one without the other. The Greeks actually *built this into* their politics, with scheduled moments of sensual abandon. It is important even today to exercise your civic duty with small acts of senseless mirth.

A cocktail downed from a salt cup is a conscious deviation from reason. Other than that, there is no spectacular rationale for putting a perfectly good cocktail into a salt cup. (Well, maybe there is, but for the sake of emphasizing the importance of being irrational, let's just say there isn't.) In fact, there is a very good reason why you should not. Any drink put into a salt cup is going to take on salt in an arc that looks like this:

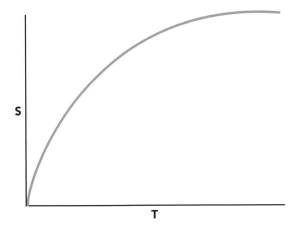

S

T

The liquid dissolves a lot of salt, quickly. This brings us to one of the three chief charms of serving a cocktail from a salt cup: You will need to drink it fast. College students have a profound understanding of the benefits of slamming drinks. Sadly, but fortunately, most of us unlearn this as we grow older. Our modern adult reason puts enduring personal health above transient social catharsis. Fair enough, but putting a cocktail in a salt cup and slamming it before it gets too salty is part of a well-balanced social calendar.

Another mixological benefit of salt cups is that salt happens to be great in a many cocktails. So the trick to using them effectively is to mix drinks that are well-suited to quick quaffing, and that also benefit from a little added salt. A shot of espresso with a half-shot of Calvados (page 209) is never drunk slowly anyway, and the touch of salt takes the bitter edge off the coffee.

Salt cups have thermal qualities as well, holding heat and cold far better than glass. Freezing, refrigerating, or heating a salt cup before serving opens new doors, and old ones, too. Few sophisticated drinkers these days will touch a daiquiri. The reason has nothing to do with an aversion to either

S = Salinity. T = Time. A drink will take on salt until it reaches about 35 percent salinity, at which point it will taste like what it is: ten times saltier than the sea. Drinks get pretty intense after 2 percent and fiercely unpalatable by the time they reach 3 percent.

lime juice or rum (both are the height of fashion these days), but rather with the sweetness and the vaguely lowbrow vibe we get from anyone drinking a cocktail that routinely comes from a slushie machine. But with an edge of salt and a mandate to slam it, a chilled daiquiri shooter in a salt cup (page 201) has a restrained salty-sweetness that is thoroughly contemporary. Downing it as a shooter can be seen as ironic and hip, or classically inspired.

A successful salt cup cocktail will embrace the three technical features salt cups have to offer: improved flavor from added salt, improved temperature from salt's thermal mass, and improved impact from expedited consumption. A fourth reason to drink from salt cups comes to mind. Salt cups are dazzling to behold, sensual to touch, and soul-stirring to ponder. What better companion for a drink?

Islay Scotch and Chocolate

Scotch is something we normally pour deliberately, while speaking in a serious voice, and then sip slowly from the glistening luxury of good crystal. Except if you're from Scotland; then you say "Get in my belly!" and down she goes. I'm not exactly sure where I sit myself: somewhere between my intellectual thirst for savored complexity and my romantic yen for slamming a shot and pouring a second one over some haggis. A little luxurious chocolate adds a childish decadence to this drink, but the wild way the salt shifts the mineral profile of the Scotch transforms it into something that needs a new tradition all its own: a sort of slammed delectation.

1 (2-ounce) Himalayan salt shot glass

¼ ounce dark chocolate (at least 64% cacao)

¼ cup peaty Scotch, such as Laphroaig

MAKES 1 SERVING

Chill the salt glass in the refrigerator for at least 30 minutes.

Meanwhile, put the chocolate in a small ramekin or bowl and seal the top with plastic wrap. Make sure the edges of the plastic are tucked tightly around the top. Put the sealed ramekin in a larger bowl filled with enough very hot tap water to come at least halfway up the side of the ramekin. Make sure the edges of the plastic are not hanging into the water. If they are, water can get into the chocolate, which will make it grainy. Set aside for 10 minutes to melt the chocolate.

Remove the bowl of chocolate from the bowl of water. Dry the bottom and sides of the chocolate bowl and then uncover. Dip the rim of the chilled salt glass into the warm chocolate, creating a thick lip of chocolate around the opening of the glass. Return the salt glass to the refrigerator for 1 minute.

Pour the Scotch into the glass and sip, licking a bit of chocolate from the rim as you proceed. Try to finish within 5 minutes or so, lest the Scotch become too salty. The last sip will be downright briny, palate-tingling, and delicious.

Double-Fisted Tecate and Mezcal

Booze is sometimes good because it is bad. Take mezcal, for example. Speed of quaffage is the one surefire way to minimize mezcal's rugged smokiness, and a frosty slug of beer to chase it down pays tribute simultaneously to the time-honored tradition of our Mexican forebears and our unbridled animal instinct to douse anything that smokes with anything liquid. Double-fist the two of them and you are merely embracing the natural order.

1 (2-ounce) Himalayan salt shot glass

¼ cup smoky mezcal, such as Zauco

1 (12-ounce) can Mexican beer, such as Tecate, chilled

MAKES 1 SERVING

Chill the salt glass in the freezer for at least 10 minutes.

Just before serving, fill the salt glass with the mezcal. Open the beer. Pick up the mezcal in one hand. Pick up the beer in the other hand. Shoot the mezcal. Drink the beer.

Rimming your Mezcal (and your can of beer) with beautiful, flaky sea salt is a great way to go. But drinking from a salt cup can be a less distracting way to savor your serious spirits.

Quick-Cured Oyster with Gin Sangrita

It's weird that an animal would offer itself to us as something to be slurped down in a single gulp, but oysters even provide us with the cup of their shell for streamlining the process, so who are we to question the natural order of things? This drink honors the oyster's oddly beverage-like oceanic flavor with a little herbaceous hooch, a splash of tart tomato, and a chilled salt cup for some cool, briny zing.

1 (2-ounce) Himalayan salt shot glass

1 small oyster, such as a Pacific oyster, in its shell

Grind of black pepper

1 lime wedge

2 tablespoons dry English-style gin, such as Plymouth

1 tablespoon vegetable juice, such as V8

MAKES 1 SERVING

Chill the salt glass in the freezer for at least 10 minutes.

Just before serving, shuck the oyster and slip it into the frozen glass; return to the freezer for 1 minute.

Grind the pepper into the glass and squeeze the lime wedge over the oyster. Swirl once. Add the gin and juice. Stir briefly. Shoot.

Iced Pepper Vodka Shooter

My dad asserts that there is only one respectable way to drink vodka. Start with a good Russian or Polish vodka (preferably potato vodka), get it bone-chillingly cold in the freezer, pour it into a shot glass, crack black pepper over it, and down she goes in one gulp. My grandparents were not vodka drinkers, and my dad spent his formative years drinking beer with poets in Bristol, England, and New York's West Village, so I have no idea how he arrived at such authority, but I've never questioned it. Until I realized it was missing salt.

1 (2-ounce) Himalayan salt shot glass

¼ cup Black Pepper Vodka (recipe follows)

A grind of black pepper

MAKES 1 SERVING

Chill the salt glass and vodka in the freezer for 24 hours.

Just before serving, fill the salt glass with the pepper vodka and grind one twist of black pepper over it. Shoot, grimace, sigh, repeat.

Black Pepper Vodka

½ cup cracked black peppercorns

2 cups potato vodka, such as Luksusowa

MAKES 2 CUPS

Combine the peppercorns and vodka in a glass jar. Seal and set aside for at least 2 hours or up to 6 hours. Strain out and discard the solids. Store in a tightly closed glass container forever, or until your father visits.

Basil Salt Daiquiri

Even though he was a master of taut prose, Ernest Hemingway was inclined toward the florid when it came to daiquiris. To the holy trinity of rum, lime, and sugar, he added the insult of maraschino liqueur and the injury of grapefruit juice. And perhaps to drown the shame of this ignominy, he decreed that his daiquiri must be served as a double. But his desire to add complexity to the original has inspired countless riffs on the classic. Salt and basil speak a complex truth about daiquiris that is happy and delicious and succinct.

1½ ounces white rum

1 ounce fresh lime juice

¼ ounce basil simple syrup (see right)

MAKES 1 DRINK

Freeze a salt cup for at least 1 hour.

To make the basil syrup, combine 24 basil leaves and 1½ cups water in a small saucepan and heat to a simmer. After the infusion reduces by half, pour the infusion through a strainer to remove the leaves, then put the infusion back into the saucepan. Add ¾ cup sugar and bring back to a simmer. Turn off the heat and allow to cool completely before using.

To make the daiquiri, combine the rum, lime juice, and basil syrup over ice. Remove the salt cup from the freezer. Shake the rum mixture well and strain into the frozen salt cup. Drink with alacrity.

Salacious Julep

The first recorded order of a julep was placed by some ladies sunning themselves outside a lavishly draped, valanced, and tasseled resort in West Virginia called The Greenbrier. These ladies of yawning lawns, absent husbands, dashing tennis pros—who were they? What were their cares, their passions? And most pressingly for me, why did they want this drink served to them in the silver cup that has helped make the drink legend? My own experience at The Greenbrier suggests only one answer: to hide just how much of the powerful drink they had imbibed. And from this hypothesis, I can only imagine that imbibe they did. The mint julep was a sophisticated invention for clandestine revelry. Drink from a frosty, salty cup and I leave it to you to imagine the revelry.

1 (4-ounce) Himalayan salt cup

Leaves from 1 mint sprig

1 tablespoon Simple Syrup (page 204)

Shaved ice

¼ cup bourbon

MAKES 1 SERVING

Chill the salt cup in the freezer for at least 1 hour.

Combine the mint leaves and the simple syrup in the bottom of the frozen salt cup. Muddle to release the flavor of the mint. Fill the cup with shaved ice and pour in the bourbon. Stir for a second. Sip with purpose. Lingering unnecessarily will make the julep briny.

Amaro Salato

Italian amaros are a type of ancient elixir made by steeping aromatic and bitter botanicals in alcohol—imagine after-dinner drinks sipped behind thick medieval walls, and that's the taste. Amaros are typically dark, dense concoctions. The sugar that is added to amaros as a foil for the delicious bitterness does little to open up their density. Sweetness brings balance, but some of the original clarity of the formulation is lost in darkness. A select few are wine-based, and that is what we are creating here, using white vermouth. Sipping homemade amaro from a salt cup unpacks the flavors that get crowded out by the sugar. Close your eyes and watch a new constellation of Mediterranean flavors phosphoresce in your mind's sky.

1 (2-ounce) Himalayan salt shot glass

1 tablespoon Simple Syrup (recipe follows)

1 teaspoon finely grated orange zest

¼ cup good dry vermouth, such as Dolin Blanc or Vya Dry or Imbue Bittersweet

4 to 8 drops orange bitters

MAKES 1 SERVING

Chill the salt glass in the freezer for at least 10 minutes.

Put the simple syrup on a small saucer and the orange zest on another small saucer. Dip the rim of the salt glass in the simple syrup and then in the orange zest. Refrigerate for a few minutes.

Just before serving, fill the salt glass with the vermouth and any remaining simple syrup. Add the bitters and stir briefly. Sip with purpose. Lingering will make the vermouth briny, transforming the drink from sweet to savory.

Simple Syrup

1 cup water

1 cup sugar

MAKES 1½ CUPS

Mix the water and sugar in a small saucepan until all the sugar is moistened. Bring to a boil over medium-high heat. Remove from the heat and let cool. Refrigerate for up to half your lifetime.

Warm Sake Shot with Daikon

Water is serious business for sake, and sakagura (sake breweries) are keenly aware of its role as the foundation for sake's flavor. The taste of water comes from the minerals that are in it, which is why we like mineral-rich spring water more than mineral-free distilled water. Every sake has a unique fingerprint written in calcium, magnesium, sodium, bicarbonate, and their kin. Sipped from a salt cup, the sake swirls a new mineral profile through its soul, shifting shapes in fun if sometimes fitful ways. Warming the sake accentuates the fiery heat of the drink, which distracts us from the seriousness underlying the dreamy sensation.

1 (2-ounce) Himalayan salt shot glass

¼ cup sake

1 (1-inch) cube peeled daikon

MAKES 1 SERVING

Place the sake and daikon into a *tokkuri* (sake server) or small cup and set in a small saucepan half filled with water. Bring the water in the saucepan to a simmer and then turn off the heat. Let the sake stand in the hot water for 1 minute, aiming to warm the sake to about 130°F.

Put the daikon in the salt shot glass and pour in the warm sake. Serve immediately. Without lingering too long, sip just slowly enough to follow the evolution of flavors as the sake picks up salt.

Xocolatl Xtabentún

The Mayans loved to party. Whether it was a rip-roaring ballgame or a ritualistic decapitation, the drink of choice was a heady blend of spices and chocolate. They likely added the ruby-rich spice called annatto to the mix purely because they enjoyed drinking what symbolically resembled the blood that accompanied all the fun. Add a little of the Mayan rum-based spirit xtabentún to make this drink into a cocktail, serve it in a salt cup for a little sanguinary exhilaration, and you really can imagine the good times. To make a virgin version of this drink, substitute water and a tablespoon of sugar for the rum.

1 (2-ounce) Himalayan salt shot glass

1 ounce dark chocolate (72% or more cacao)

2 tablespoons Spicy Spiced Rum (recipe follows)

MAKES 1 SERVING

Melt the chocolate in the top of a small double boiler set over barely simmering water. Stir in the spiced rum and whisk to combine. Pour into the salt glass and slurp.

Spicy Spiced Rum

2 cups dark rum

12 star anise pods, crushed

12 cardamom pods, crushed

½ guajillo chile, seeds removed, chopped

1 vanilla bean, split

1 tablespoon honey

MAKES 2 CUPS

Mix the rum, anise, cardamom, chile, vanilla bean, and honey together in a glass jar. Seal and set aside for at least 6 hours or up to 2 days.

Strain out and discard the solids. Store the spiced rum in a tightly closed glass container forever, or until drained.

Café Calva

Few things are more terrifying than seeing a truck barreling down toward you on a narrow European road at six o'clock in the morning. It's not terrifying because the road is narrow and dark and you are already clipping the shrubs with your right-side rearview mirror. It's terrifying because you know there's a likelihood that the truck driver's nervous system is a crazy mess of cigarettes and espresso fortified with a shot of brandy. The highways of Europe are defined by this dubious drink—from the café calva of France to the café corretto of Italy to the kaffekask of Sweden, there is no respite. The Catalonians' name for it, carajillo, actually means "drinking and dashing." I drink mine in the safety of my home, but from a salt cup to remind me of the taste of biting my lip as the truck miraculously passes me and vanishes into the morning.

1 (4-ounce) Himalayan salt cup

1 tablespoon sugar

1 double-shot hot espresso

1 tablespoon Calvados, grappa, or other brandy

MAKES 1 SERVING

Place the sugar in a small skillet and cook over medium-high heat until the sugar begins to melt at the edges, about 3 minutes. Continue to cook, stirring, until the sugar is uniformly golden brown and smooth, 5 to 6 minutes.

Carefully dip the rim of the salt cup into the caramel. Set aside until the sugar firms, about 1 minute.

Pour the freshly pulled espresso into the cup. Stir in the Calvados. Serve immediately. Sip with purpose. Lingering unnecessarily will make the coffee overly salty.

METRIC CONVERSIONS AND EQUIVALENTS

To Convert	Multiply
Ounces to grams	Ounces by 28.35
Pounds to kilograms	Pounds by 0.454
Teaspoons to milliliters	Teaspoons by 4.93
Tablespoons to milliliters	Tablespoons by 14.79
Fluid ounces to milliliters	Fluid ounces by 29.57
Cups to milliliters	Cups by 236.59
Cups to liters	Cups by 0.236
Pints to liters	Pints by 0.473
Quarts to liters	Quarts by 0.946
Gallons to liters	Gallons by 3.785
Inches to centimeters	Inches by 2.54

APPROXIMATE METRIC EQUIVALENTS

Volume

¼ teaspoon	1 milliliter
½ teaspoon	2.5 milliliters
¾ teaspoon	4 milliliters
1 teaspoon	5 milliliters
1¼ teaspoons	6 milliliters
1½ teaspoons	7.5 milliliters
1¾ teaspoons	8.5 milliliters
2 teaspoons	10 milliliters
1 tablespoon (½ fluid ounce)	15 milliliters
2 tablespoons (1 fluid ounce)	30 milliliters
¼ cup	60 milliliters
⅓ cup	80 milliliters
½ cup (4 fluid ounces)	120 milliliters
⅔ cup	160 milliliters
¾ cup	180 milliliters
1 cup (8 fluid ounces)	240 milliliters
1¼ cups	300 milliliters
1½ cups (12 fluid ounces)	360 milliliters
1⅔ cups	400 milliliters
2 cups (1 pint)	460 milliliters
3 cups	700 milliliters
4 cups (1 quart)	0.95 liter
1 quart plus ¼ cup	1 liter
4 quarts (1 gallon)	3.8 liters

Weight

¼ ounce	7 grams
½ ounce	14 grams
¾ ounce	21 grams
1 ounce	28 grams
1¼ ounces	35 grams
1½ ounces	42.5 grams
1⅔ ounces	45 grams
2 ounces	57 grams
3 ounces	85 grams
4 ounces (¼ pound)	113 grams
5 ounces	142 grams
6 ounces	170 grams
7 ounces	198 grams
8 ounces (½ pound)	227 grams
16 ounces (1 pound)	454 grams
35¼ ounces (2.2 pounds)	1 kilogram

Length

⅛ inch	3 millimeters
¼ inch	6 millimeters
½ inch	1.25 centimeters
1 inch	2.5 centimeters
2 inches	5 centimeters
2½ inches	6 centimeters
4 inches	10 centimeters
5 inches	13 centimeters
6 inches	15.25 centimeters
12 inches (1 foot)	30 centimeters

OVEN TEMPERATURES

To convert Fahrenheit to Celsius, subtract 32 from Fahrenheit, multiply the result by 5, then divide by 9.

Description	Fahrenheit	Celsius	British Gas Mark
Very cool	200°	95°	0
Very cool	225°	110°	¼
Very cool	250°	120°	½
Cool	275°	135°	1
Cool	300°	150°	2
Warm	325°	165°	3
Moderate	350°	175°	4
Moderately hot	375°	190°	5
Fairly hot	400°	200°	6
Hot	425°	220°	7
Very hot	450°	230°	8
Very hot	475°	245°	9

Common Ingredients and Their Approximate Equivalents

1 cup uncooked rice = 225 grams

1 cup all-purpose flour = 140 grams

1 stick butter (4 ounces • ½ cup • 8 tablespoons) = 110 grams

1 cup butter (8 ounces • 2 sticks • 16 tablespoons) = 220 grams

1 cup brown sugar, firmly packed = 225 grams

1 cup granulated sugar = 200 grams

Information compiled from a variety of sources, including *Recipes into Type* by Joan Whitman and Dolores Simon (Newton, MA: Biscuit Books, 2000); *The New Food Lover's Companion* by Sharon Tyler Herbst (Hauppauge, NY: Barron's, 1995); and *Rosemary Brown's Big Kitchen Instruction Book* (Kansas City, MO: Andrews McMeel, 1998).

INDEX